TODDLER meal PLANNER

Nicola Graimes

This is a Parragon Book

First published in 2001

Parragon
Queen Street House
4 Queen Street
Bath, BA1 1HE UK

Designed by THE BRIDGEWATER BOOK COMPANY

Art Director Terry Jeavons
Editorial Director Fiona Biggs
Senior Designer Colin Fielder
Editor Sarah Bragginton
Page Layout Jane and Chris Lanaway
Picture Research Liz Moore
Photography David Jordan
Home Economist Sarah Lewis
Illustrations Rhian Nest-James

Printed and bound in Spain

ISBN 0-75255-206-6

This book uses metric and imperial measurements. Follow the same units of measurement throughout; do not mix metric and imperial. All spoon measurements are level: teaspoons are assumed to be 5 ml and tablespoons are assumed to be 15 ml. Unless otherwise stated, milk is assumed to be full fat, eggs and individual vegetables such as potatoes are medium, and pepper is freshly ground black pepper.

The times given for each recipe are an approximate guide only because the preparation times may differ according to the techniques used by different people and the cooking times may vary as a result of the type of oven used.

contents

Introduction

It is perfectly common for a toddler's food preferences to change – even on a daily basis. Babies who previously ate just about anything you offered may start to develop apparently peculiar likes and dislikes. This is the age group where mealtimes can become a challenge – though with the right approach, you can minimise any hiccups!

If your toddler happily eats everything that is presented before him or her, then you are an incredibly lucky parent. Most of us are much less fortunate. Nevertheless, so long as you are prepared for the ups and downs, this can be a fun and rewarding time. At this stage, weaning should be firmly established – your toddler can now eat the same foods as you, usually making it unnecessary to prepare separate meals. Additionally, sterilising eating utensils and puréeing foods are now in the distant past (although good hygiene practises are still absolutely crucial).

Most importantly, don't worry if your toddler refuses to try some foods. However stressful mealtimes can be, it's vital for you to keep calm and be patient. Toddlers have an uncanny ability to pick up on their parent's anxieties and mealtimes can become battles of will. Most toddlers can be very fickle; their likes and dislikes can change, even on a daily basis, which can be extremely frustrating if you've spent time and energy lovingly preparing home-cooked food, but it's crucial not to try and force your child to eat as this can affect their attitude to food later in life.

Toddlers have a strong desire for independence and mealtimes can be a perfect time to exercise it. At this stage, it is important to nurture and encourage this

ABOVE *It's fun for your child to help you with meals and learn about how food makes its way to the table.*

LEFT *Your toddler will now want to use his or her own cutlery – encourage this growing self-confidence in your child.*

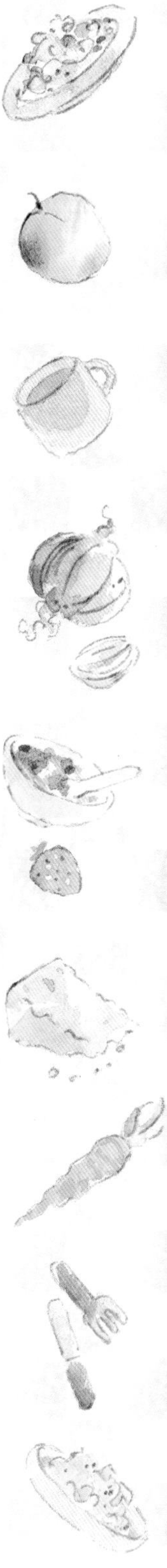

growing sense of self. Allow your child to feed him or herself or at least offer a second spoon – it's all part of the fun! By doing so, you are preparing your toddler for times ahead: for example, starting nursery or school.

The aim of this book is to ease any anxieties you may have about meals and mealtimes, and smooth the transition from toddler to young child. The recipes have been designed to appeal to young children and adults alike, with the odd concession to nutritious versions of so-called 'children's food'. I've tried to include a wide range of dishes, incorporating a variety of cuisines, flavours and textures. The meal plans will help you to balance your child's diet on a daily and weekly basis. Treat these as guidelines – you don't have to stick to them rigidly.

It's easy to become bogged down in the intricacies of providing a balanced diet, but good, nutritious food does not have to be complicated to prepare or take long to cook. Nothing could be easier than a baked potato with a dollop of pesto or houmus. Canned beans, such as chickpeas or kidney beans, and frozen vegetables, including spinach and peas, add substance and nutritional value to soups, stews, risottos and pasta dishes. Conjure up different ways of serving vegetables. Often raw vegetables are more popular than cooked, and they're healthier. Additionally, if time allows, encourage your toddler to join in the cooking – I've found they're more likely to try the results. Food should be fun; after all, eating is one of the great pleasures in life!

What Does My Toddler Need?

Children over a year old can join in family meals, but their requirement for high-energy foods is still much greater than that of adults. Compared with the very rapid growth rate during the first year, your toddler is now growing more slowly. However, you'll find that he or she is far more active – walking, jumping and running – which means that extra calories and a varied, nutritious diet are essential for growth and proper development.

The term 'balanced diet' can intimidate even the most nutritionally aware parent. Yet as long as your toddler is eating a good mix of foods, including bread, pasta, rice, potatoes, fruits and vegetables, dairy foods, meat, fish and eggs, preferably on a daily or, if not, on a weekly basis, then that should be more than sufficient. Obviously this range of foods can vary depending on special diets, eating preferences and the presence of any food intolerances or allergies. Choose foods from the food groups below and your toddler will almost certainly be getting all the nutrients he or she needs.

STARCHY FOODS

Starchy foods, otherwise known as carbohydrates, include breakfast cereals, bread, pasta, rice and potatoes. These should form a major part of your

LEFT *Offer raw vegetables and fruit as a snack instead of biscuits or cake.*

ABOVE *Your child will become increasingly active and have high energy levels.*

toddler's diet as they are a good source of energy, fibre, vitamins and minerals. Wholegrain varieties, such as wholemeal bread, brown rice and pasta, provide the richest source of nutrients and fibre, yet should not be given in large amounts to young children. Unlike adults, toddlers find it difficult to digest large amounts of high-fibre foods, leading to stomach upsets and a reduced appetite. Fibre can also interfere with the absorption of certain minerals.

FRUITS AND VEGETABLES

Fresh and frozen fruits and vegetables, more so than tinned, are an essential part of a toddler's diet, providing rich amounts of vitamins, minerals and fibre. Try to offer around four to five different types of fresh produce a day, such as citrus fruit, salad, and orange, red and green vegetables, to ensure a good balance of vitamins.

Many children refuse to eat cooked vegetables – mainly because of their different texture – but will happily try raw sticks of carrot, red pepper and celery or lightly steamed mangetout, baby sweetcorn and broccoli, especially if dipped in houmus, guacamole, garlic butter or mayonnaise. Presenting vegetables in various guises also seems to work. Try them puréed in soups and sauces, combined with mashed potatoes or grated into patties or burgers.

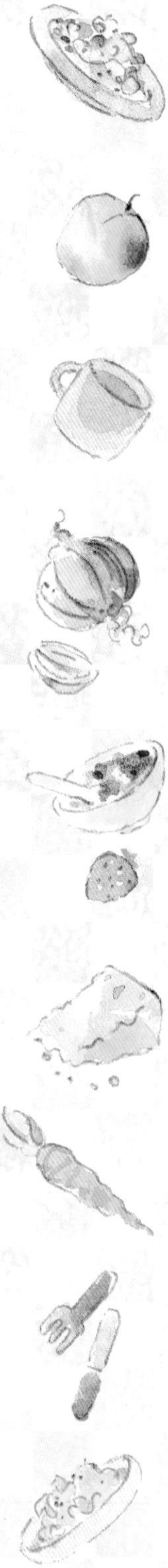

ABOVE *Milk still forms an important part of a toddler's diet: cow's milk is fine too.*

MEAT, FISH, EGGS AND VEGETARIAN ALTERNATIVES

Your toddler requires some of these protein foods at every main meal, but it is vital to offer a good variety, including beans, lentils and soya-based foods. Protein foods are essential for growth and development and are also incredibly versatile, lending themselves to a variety of dishes.

DAIRY FOODS

Milk, cheese and yogurt provide protein, vitamins and minerals, particularly calcium for healthy bones and teeth. Although cow's milk can be used in cooking from 6 months, it's suitable as a drink from 1 year. Opt for full-cream dairy produce because it provides the fat and therefore the energy required by your growing child. If your toddler is eating well, then you can switch to semi-skimmed milk from 2 years. Experts recommend that children under 5 have 600 ml/1 pint of milk a day, although some of this can be poured over breakfast cereals or offered in the form of sauces and milky puddings.

SUGARY FOODS

Young children naturally have a sweet tooth and it's easy to pander to this preference. Unfortunately, sugary foods, including chocolate, sweets, cakes, biscuits and fizzy drinks, rot the teeth and spoil a child's appetite for healthier alternatives. It can be a challenge to curb a child's desire for sweet foods, especially when presented with aisles of sugary delights while food shopping, but try to start as you mean to go on. Look for healthier alternatives to the above, but don't resort to those containing artificial sweeteners, since they've been found to cause upset stomachs if eaten in excess. Nevertheless, an outright ban on sweet foods can backfire, making them even more desirable to your toddler: as in most things, the answer seems to be to offer sugary things in moderation.

IRON

Iron deficiency is particularly common, especially among women and children. The mineral is essential for the healthy development of mind and body and a deficiency can lead to tiredness, irritability, anaemia and a poor immune system. Iron absorption can be enhanced by accompanying a meal with a glass of fresh orange juice. Red meat and liver, fish, eggs, beans and lentils, some fruits and vegetables, wholegrain cereals, fortified breakfast cereals and dried fruit are all good sources of iron.

FATTY FOODS

Children need a higher proportion of fat in their diets than adults, both for energy and development. This does not mean that children thrive on high-fat pastries, biscuits, cakes, crisps and fried foods, but do try, at least up to the age of 5, to offer full-fat dairy products, oils of vegetable origin, lean meat, skinless chicken and oily fish such as salmon, tuna, mackerel, sardines and herrings. Avoid hydrogenated fats, found in many processed foods, including pies, sausages and biscuits, since they are just as bad for us as saturated fats. Grilling, poaching and baking foods are preferable.

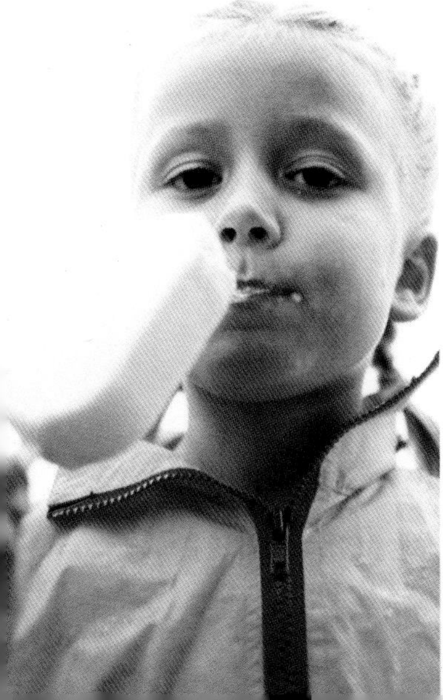

SALTY FOODS

Cut down on salt as much as possible, especially as this seasoning is found naturally in many foods and is also added to many commercial products. If cooking for the whole family, remove your child's portion before adding any salt.

LEFT *Toddlers naturally have a sweet tooth, but try to offer sugary foods in moderation.*

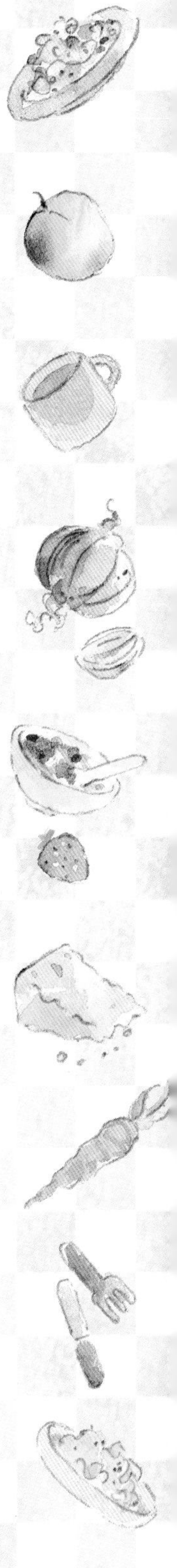

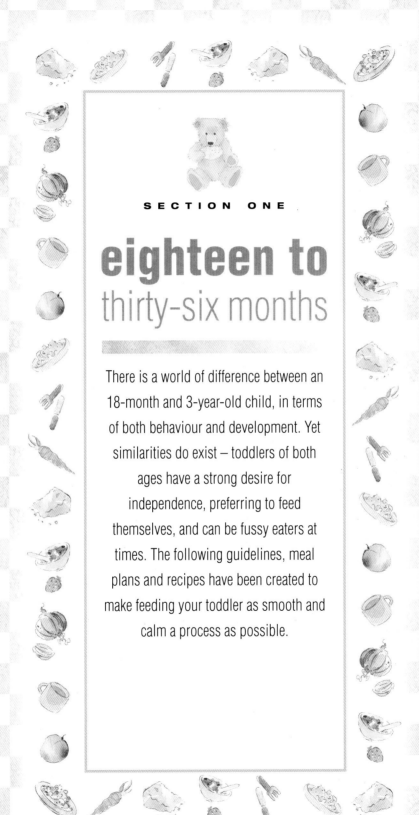

SECTION ONE

eighteen to thirty-six months

There is a world of difference between an 18-month and 3-year-old child, in terms of both behaviour and development. Yet similarities do exist – toddlers of both ages have a strong desire for independence, preferring to feed themselves, and can be fussy eaters at times. The following guidelines, meal plans and recipes have been created to make feeding your toddler as smooth and calm a process as possible.

Good Eating Habits

Many nutritionists believe that good eating habits are formed in early childhood, so it is essential to encourage your toddler to try (and enjoy) a variety of foods, encompassing a range of flavours, colours and textures, when he or she is as young as possible. However, it's never too late to make healthy changes to your toddler's diet.

FRESH IS BEST

In an ideal world, only home-cooked foods would pass our little ones' lips, yet this is unrealistic for most us. The biggest influence on our children's health is the quality and variety of ingredients used and, perhaps reassuringly, not all prepared foods are bad. The foods you should avoid are those where saturated or hydrogenated fats, colourings, additives, sweeteners, sugar and salt appear high in the ingredients list. Try to get into the habit of reading the list of ingredients and the nutritional information on the packet before you buy it.

Having said this, a toddler's diet shouldn't rely on processed foods, and it is crucial to introduce freshly prepared meals at as young an age as possible. Habits are formed early and it's easier to avoid junk foods while children are small. Toddlers will inevitably turn their noses up at some foods, but the more choice they are given, the better – both for them and for you.

Researchers at the University of Birmingham have found that young children are more open to new tastes and flavours than is sometimes assumed. Additionally, fresh foods don't have to take long to prepare, usually taste better than junk foods, and are more nutritious. If this wasn't enough to convince you, they're usually cheaper: with convenience foods you are actually paying for someone else to do the work for you!

EATING TOGETHER

There are numerous reasons why it is not always possible for the family to eat together. However, you'll reap the benefits in the long term, even if you manage communal mealtimes only at the weekend. For the rest of the week, try at least to sit down with your toddler while he or she

ABOVE If you eat plenty of fresh fruit, your children should follow by example and accept this as normal.

is eating, and perhaps have your own small portion of food. Toddlers learn by example and it also makes mealtimes a more enjoyable and social affair. Incidentally, try to ignore poor eating habits and you'll probably find your toddler will soon get bored with playing up. Instead, offer heaps of praise and encouragement when your toddler eats well.

SNACK TIME

While some toddlers refuse to eat a complete meal, most relish snacks, especially if they can feed themselves. Take advantage of this by offering healthy snacks – this may be a way of supplementing an otherwise restricted diet. The following ideas may help when you are faced with a hungry toddler:

- Wedges of raw fruit and vegetables
- Rice cakes with low-salt yeast extract
- Slices of pitta bread with smooth peanut butter
- Fruit muffins with banana
- Natural yogurt with honey
- Breadsticks with houmus
- Soft tortilla with guacamole
- Flapjacks
- Fruit scones
- Homemade popcorn
- Fingers of pineapple with cream cheese
- Homemade vegetable crisps
- Dried fruit and nuts
- Carrot cake
- Low-salt tortilla chips, covered with grated cheese and grilled
- Oatcakes and pâté

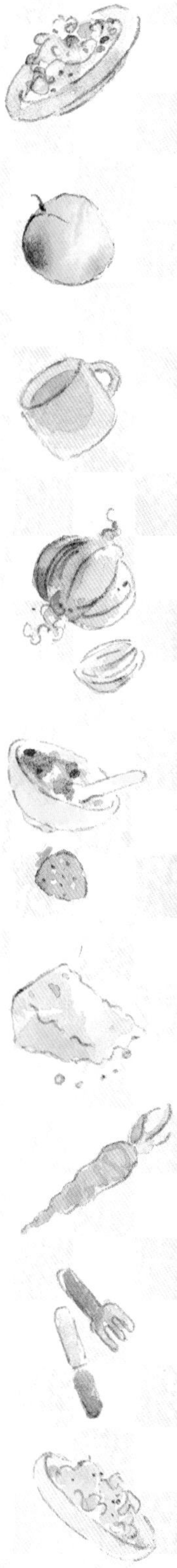

Establishing a Routine

All toddlers are different – some take to eating three main meals a day, others prefer to snack. Both are acceptable at this stage, although, as your toddler becomes older, it is advisable to introduce a pattern of regular eating times. Try to make mealtimes fun and not a time of conflict.

THREE MEALS A DAY

Work on establishing a regular eating pattern, based on three main meals, plus a couple of snacks a day. Even this can take time and patience to establish, however, so don't despair. If 'grazing' is preferred by your toddler, make sure that he or she is offered a varied selection of healthy snacks (see page 13) based on high-energy foods.

Toddlers have small stomachs and require regular small meals to keep them going. Don't worry if he or she sometimes doesn't seem hungry, or even skips a meal: as long as your toddler is gaining weight and also growing and developing well, then there should be no need for concern.

A healthy diet should be based on fruits and vegetables, bread, pasta, rice, potatoes, breakfast

LEFT *Replace some of your child's milk intake with home-made fruit smoothies or unsweetened fruit juice.*

cereals, meat, fish, eggs and full-fat dairy produce, with the occasional sweet treat. You may obviously have to make allowances for personal preferences and special diets.

There is now no need to purée or mash foods – your toddler should be getting used to, or be familiar with, chewing and with the sometimes unfamiliar texture of solid foods. Some young children dislike lumps, whether meat, fruit or vegetables, and mincing or finely chopping such foods may make them acceptable.

PRESENTATION

Imaginative and attractive presentation can make the difference between a toddler eating or refusing to even try a meal. This doesn't mean that you have to spend hours painstakingly arranging every meal on the plate, but try to make meals look as inviting as possible. Bright colours, different textures and a range of shapes make all the difference, as do interesting plates, eating utensils, bibs and mats.

DRINKS

Milk should still form an important part of your child's diet, since it provides a valuable combination of energy, protein, calcium, iron, zinc and vitamins. Cola, fizzy drinks, tea, coffee and sweetened fruit juices and squash should be avoided if possible. Sugar-laden drinks rot the teeth, curb the appetite and lead to weight gain. However, low-sugar alternatives that contain artificial sweeteners are often no better, and can upset the stomach if drunk in excess. Water, diluted unsweetened fruit juices and home-made versions are the preferred option. Smoothies, made from puréed fruit, milk and/or yogurt, freshly squeezed juices and home-made hot chocolate (cubes of good-quality chocolate melted into hot milk) all make nutritious, comforting drinks that are not full of sugar and additives.

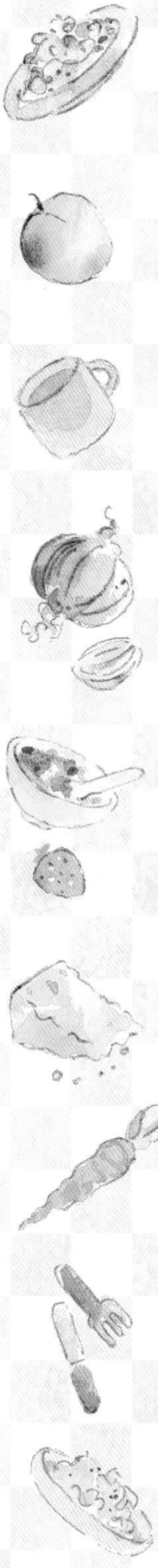

MEAL PLANNER 1

18-36 MONTHS	BREAKFAST	LUNCH
Day 1	Ready Brek, toast, milk	Smoked salmon & broccoli pasta Baked peach crumbles
Day 2	Boiled egg, toast, melon, milk	Rice balls with tomato sauce Vegetables Banana custard scrunch
Day 3	Weetabix and banana Fruit bread, milk	Starfish pie, peas Baked apple & custard
Day 4	Porridge & grated apple Toast, milk	Pork & apple casserole Potatoes & vegetables Fromage frais
Day 5	Pancakes with fruit filling Yogurt, milk	Bubble & squeak patties Peas and grilled sausage Ice cream
Day 6	Cereal & raisins, toast, milk	Pasta and vegetables in cheese sauce Baked peach crumbles
Day 7	Diced bacon & grilled tomatoes on toast Yogurt, milk	Roast (or vegetarian alternative), roast potatoes and vegetables Rice pudding with raisins

TEA	SUPPER
Pizza fingers Houmus & vegetable sticks Yogurt	Sardines on toast Fruit Milky drink
Chicken fingers & coleslaw Strawberry & vanilla ice	Cheese on toast Fruit Milky drink
Bean & pasta soup Garlic bread Chocolate muffin	Sandwich Fruit Milky drink
Baked potato with tuna & sweetcorn Strawberry ice lolly	Scrambled egg with muffin Fruit & milky drink
Eggy bread and beans Flapjack	Guacamole with tortilla/pitta bread Vegetable sticks Fruit & milky drink
Rice balls/chicken sticks with houmus and tortilla Coleslaw Strawberry yogurt ice	Sandwich Fruit Milky drink
Tuna and cheese on toast Vegetable sticks Banana custard scrunch	Apple muffins Fruit Milky drink

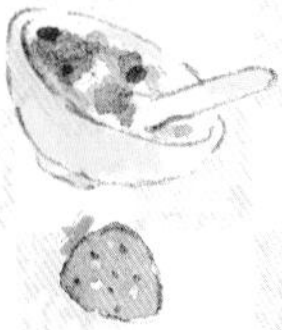

Hearty Bean & Pasta Soup

PREPARATION TIME *10 minutes* **COOKING TIME** *40 minutes*

FREEZING *suitable, but omit Parmesan cheese* **SERVES** *4 adults*

This wholesome bean and pasta soup is substantial enough to be served as a meal in itself, providing a good, healthy balance of vegetables and pasta. Accompany it with buttery garlic bread.

INGREDIENTS
4 tbsp olive oil
1 onion, finely chopped
1 celery stick, chopped
1 carrot, peeled and diced
1 bay leaf
1.2 litres/2 pints vegetable stock
400 g/14 oz can chopped tomatoes
175 g/6 oz pasta shapes, such as farfalle, shells or twists
400-g/14-oz can cannellini beans, drained and rinsed
salt and freshly ground black pepper
200 g/7 oz spinach or chard, thick stalks removed and shredded
40 g/1½ oz Parmesan cheese, finely grated

❶ Heat the olive oil in a large, heavy-based saucepan. Add the onion, celery and carrot and cook over a medium heat for 8–10 minutes, stirring occasionally, until the vegetables have softened.

❷ Add the bay leaf, stock and chopped tomatoes, then bring to the boil. Reduce the heat, cover and simmer for 15 minutes, or until the vegetables are tender.

❸ Add the pasta and beans, then bring the soup back to the boil and simmer for 10 minutes, or until the pasta is just tender. Stir occasionally to prevent the pasta sticking to the bottom of the pan and burning.

❹ Season to taste, add the spinach and cook for a further 2 minutes, or until tender. Serve, sprinkled with Parmesan cheese.

Creamy Smoked Salmon & Broccoli Pasta

PREPARATION TIME *10 minutes* **COOKING TIME** *15 minutes*
FREEZING *unsuitable* **SERVES** *4 adults*

Smoked salmon pieces are now readily available in supermarkets and fishmongers and don't cost the earth. It is ideal for this dish as it has a slightly milder flavour and loses its oily texture when cooked, which seems to appeal to children.

INGREDIENTS
400 g/14 oz pasta shells, bows or tagliatelle
225 g/8 oz broccoli florets
1 tbsp olive oil
2 tbsp butter
1 leek, finely chopped
200 g tub garlic and herb cream cheese
6 tbsp whole milk
100 g/3½ oz smoked salmon pieces
salt and freshly ground black pepper

❶ Cook the pasta according to the instructions on the packet, until the pasta is tender, then drain. Meanwhile, steam the broccoli for 8–10 minutes, or until tender.

❷ At the same time, prepare the sauce. Heat the oil and butter in a small heavy-based frying pan, then add the leek and sauté for 7 minutes, or until softened. Gently stir in the cream cheese and milk and heat through.

❸ Add the smoked salmon pieces and cook for a minute or so, until they turn opaque. Combine the sauce with the pasta and broccoli and mix together well. Season.

Pizza Fingers

PREPARATION TIME *15 minutes* **COOKING TIME** *25 minutes*
FREEZING *suitable* **SERVES** *2 adults*

This pizza is sliced into handy-sized pieces, which are perfect for little fingers to hold. I've given a choice of four toppings to give the pizza a chequerboard effect, but you can opt for one topping if preferred. Additionally, a ready-made foccacia or ciabatta is a good alternative to a home-made base.

❶ To make the pizza base, place the flour, salt and yeast in a bowl. Make a well in the centre of the flour and add the water and oil, then mix with a knife until the mixture forms a soft dough.

❷ Turn out onto a lightly floured work surface and knead for 5 minutes. Cover and leave for 5 minutes. Knead again for a further 5 minutes until the dough is elastic. Place in a lightly oiled bowl and cover with clingfilm. Leave in a warm place for 45 minutes, or until doubled in size.

❸ Preheat the oven to 220°C/425°F/Gas Mark 7. To make the tomato sauce, heat the oil in a heavy-based frying pan and fry the garlic for 1 minute, or until softened. Add the passata and sugar, then cook for 5–7 minutes, until reduced and thickened. Stir in the oregano and seasoning, then set aside.

INGREDIENTS

- 2 tsp olive oil, plus extra for greasing and sprinkling
- 1 clove garlic, crushed
- 140 g/5 oz passata
- ½ tsp sugar
- ½ tsp oregano
- salt and freshly ground black pepper
- 115 g/4 oz mozzarella cheese
- 85 g/3 oz Cheddar cheese, grated

PIZZA BASE

- 225 g/8 oz strong white flour, sifted
- 1 tsp salt
- ½ tsp easy-blend yeast
- 150 ml/5 fl oz warm water
- 1 tbsp olive oil

TOPPINGS

- Handful of cooked fresh spinach leaves, tough stalks removed, shredded and squeezed dry
- 75 g/2¾ oz canned tuna in oil, drained
- ½ yellow or orange pepper, seeded and finely sliced
- 4 slices salami

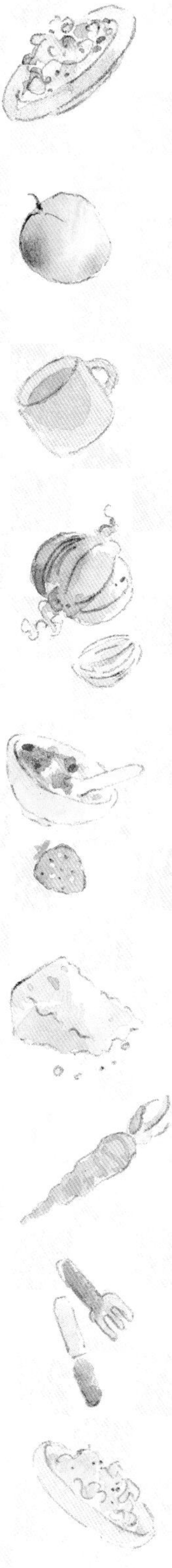

4 Knead the risen dough lightly, then roll out to form a rough rectangle or place in an oiled rectangular-shaped tin. If you are not using a tin, place the base on a lightly oiled baking sheet and push up the edges of the dough to form a shallow rim.

5 Spoon the tomato mixture over the base. Top one quarter of the base with the cooked spinach, a second quarter with tuna, a third quarter with the yellow pepper and the remaining quarter with salami. Crumble the mozzarella cheese with your fingers and sprinkle it over the toppings. Repeat with the Cheddar cheese. Season and drizzle with a little olive oil.

6 Bake in the top of the oven for 12–15 minutes, until the topping is slightly crisp and golden. Slice into fingers before serving.

Pork & Apple Casserole

PREPARATION TIME *10 minutes* **COOKING TIME** *1 hour, 18 minutes*

FREEZING *suitable* **SERVES** *4 adults*

The apple adds a delicious sweetness and texture to this warming casserole, packed with tender pork pieces. It is a big hit served with a dollop of mashed potato or plain rice.

INGREDIENTS
1 tbsp olive oil
4 boneless pork loins, each weighing about 115 g/4 oz
2 leeks, finely sliced
2 carrots, peeled and finely chopped
1 tbsp plain flour
200 ml/7 fl oz vegetable stock
75 ml/2½ fl oz apple juice
2 tsp Dijon mustard
1 bay leaf
1 tbsp fresh rosemary, finely chopped
2 eating apples, peeled, cored and sliced
salt and freshly ground black pepper

❶ Preheat the oven to 180°C/350°F/Gas Mark 4.

❷ Heat the oil in a heavy-based frying pan. Add the pork and cook for 5 minutes, until brown. Transfer to a casserole dish.

❸ Add the leeks to the pan and sauté for 5 minutes, or until softened, then add the carrots. Cook for a further 3 minutes, covered. Add the flour and cook for 1 minute, stirring well.

❹ Gradually add the stock, apple juice, mustard, bay leaf and rosemary. Bring to the boil and cook for 2 minutes, stirring until thickened. Season to taste.

❺ Arrange the apple slices on top of the pork and pour the sauce over the top. Cover and cook for about 1 hour, or until the pork is tender.

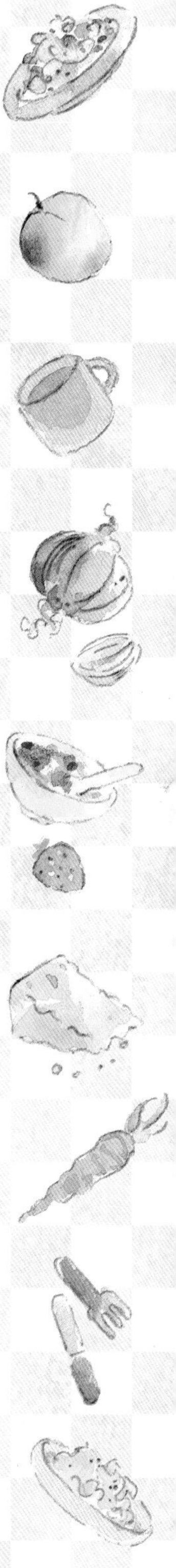

Crispy Chicken Fingers with Garlic Dip

PREPARATION TIME *15 minutes* **COOKING TIME** *8 minutes*

FREEZING *suitable* **MAKES** *6 fingers*

These polenta-encrusted chicken pieces are perfect finger food for toddlers, and they seem to enjoy dipping them into the garlic dip! Serve the goujons with the crunchy nut coleslaw (see page 26).

INGREDIENTS
20 g/¾ oz fine cornmeal or polenta
½ tsp paprika
salt and freshly ground black pepper
175 g/6 oz skinless chicken breast, cut into strips
1 tbsp olive oil
1 egg, beaten
vegetable oil, for shallow frying

GARLIC DIP
6 tbsp mayonnaise
1 small clove garlic, crushed
good squeeze of fresh lemon juice

❶ First make the garlic dip. Put the mayonnaise, garlic and lemon juice into a bowl and mix well.

❷ Put the cornmeal, paprika and seasoning in a shallow bowl. Dip each piece of chicken into the olive oil, then the egg. Roll the chicken in the cornmeal mixture and shake to remove any crumbs.

❸ Heat enough oil to generously cover a heavy-based frying pan. Arrange the chicken in the pan and fry for 2–3 minutes on each side, until cooked and golden.

Starfish Pie

PREPARATION TIME *10 minutes*
COOKING TIME *45 minutes*
FREEZING *suitable*
SERVES *4 adults*

Golden puff-pastry shapes add a fun element to this creamy fish pie, but you can opt for mashed potato if preferred. It's wise to sift through the pie with a fork before serving to ensure there are no stray bones.

INGREDIENTS
2 hard-boiled eggs
1 tbsp olive oil
1 onion, finely chopped
1 celery stick, finely chopped
1 carrot, peeled and finely chopped
small handful of spinach leaves, tough stalks removed and finely shredded
250 ml/8 fl oz full-cream milk
4 tbsp double cream
55 g/2 oz mature Cheddar cheese, grated
1 tsp Dijon mustard
2 tbsp finely chopped fresh parsley
squeeze of fresh lemon juice
salt and freshly ground black pepper
225 g/8 oz undyed smoked haddock, skin and bones removed, cut into pieces
225 g/8 oz cod fillet, skin and bones removed
1 sheet of ready-rolled puff pastry, defrosted if using frozen
1 egg, beaten, to glaze

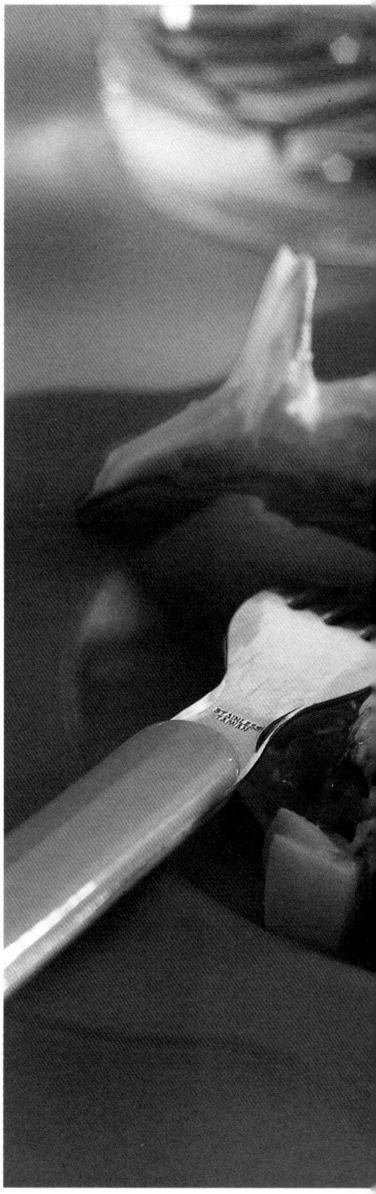

1. Preheat the oven to 200°C/400°F/Gas Mark 6.

2. Heat the oil in a heavy-based frying pan. Add the onion and sauté for 5 minutes, or until softened, then add the celery and carrot and sauté for 3 minutes. Add the spinach and cook for a further 2 minutes, or until tender.

❸ Stir in the milk and cream and bring to the boil. Turn off the heat and stir in the Cheddar cheese, mustard, parsley and lemon juice. Season to taste.

❹ Place the fish in an ovenproof dish. Peel and chop the egg and spoon it over the fish, then top with the creamy vegetable sauce.

❺ Place the pastry on a lightly floured work surface. Make fish and starfish shapes using biscuit cutters, then arrange them on top of the fish pie. Brush the pastry shapes with beaten egg and bake for 20–25 minutes, or until the fish is cooked and the pastry shapes have risen and are a golden brown colour.

Crunchy Nut Coleslaw

PREPARATION TIME *10 minutes* **COOKING TIME** *1 minute*
FREEZING *unsuitable* **SERVES** *2 adults*

The natural sweetness of the fruit in this pretty pink salad makes it appealing to toddlers. The spring onion is optional and can be added if your child likes it. The coleslaw goes particularly well with the chicken fingers (page 23).

❶ Mix together the ingredients for the dressing in a small bowl.

❷ Place the sunflower seeds in a dry frying pan and cook for a minute or so until they are a light golden brown colour.

❸ Put the cabbage, carrot, apple and spring onion, if using, in a serving bowl. Add the sunflower seeds and mix until all the ingredients are combined.

❹ Spoon over the dressing and stir to coat the salad.

INGREDIENTS
2 tbsp sunflower seeds
½ small red cabbage, grated
1 large carrot, peeled and grated
½ apple, cored and diced
1 spring onion, finely sliced (optional)

DRESSING
3 tbsp mayonnaise
1 tsp white wine vinegar, according to taste
2 tbsp natural yogurt
salt and freshly ground black pepper

Bubble & Squeak Patties

PREPARATION TIME *15 minutes* **COOKING TIME** *40 minutes*
FREEZING *suitable* **SERVES** *4 adults*

These patties are a great way of getting children to eat cabbage! They are delicious with a fresh tomato sauce and an egg on top.

INGREDIENTS
700 g/1 lb 9 oz potatoes, peeled and cut into even-sized pieces
300 g/10½ oz Savoy or green cabbage, finely shredded
1 tbsp olive oil
1 onion, finely chopped
1 tsp Dijon mustard
85 g/3 oz mature Cheddar cheese, grated
1 egg, beaten
salt and freshly ground black pepper
flour, for dusting
vegetable oil, for frying

❶ Cook the potatoes in salted boiling water for 15 minutes, or until tender. Drain well.

❷ Meanwhile, steam the cabbage for 5–8 minutes, or until tender.

❸ While the potatoes and cabbage are cooking, heat the oil in a heavy-based frying pan. Fry the onion for 5–8 minutes.

❹ Place the potatoes and cabbage in a large bowl and mash using a potato masher. Add the onion, mustard, Cheddar, egg and seasoning and mix well with a wooden spoon until all the ingredients are combined. Leave to cool, or until the mixture is cool enough to handle.

❺ Flour a large plate and your hands and shape the mixture into 8 patties. Heat enough oil to cover the base of a large frying pan and fry the patties in batches over a medium heat for 3–4 minutes on each side.

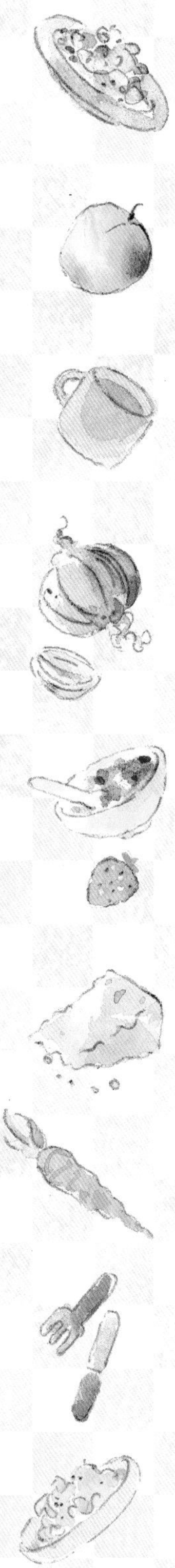

Spicy Rice Balls with Tomato Sauce

PREPARATION TIME *15 minutes, plus 30 minutes cooling*

COOKING TIME *30 minutes* **FREEZING** *suitable* **SERVES** *4 adults*

These delicately spiced rice balls are similar to falafel but have a lighter texture. I've used arborio rice because its sticky texture helps the balls hold together, but any type of cooked rice is suitable for this recipe. You can serve them wrapped in a warm tortilla with houmus, instead of the tomato sauce, if liked.

INGREDIENTS
85 g/3 oz arborio rice
300 ml/10 fl oz vegetable stock
1 tbsp olive oil
1 onion, finely chopped
2 cloves garlic, finely chopped
1 tsp ground cumin
1 tsp ground coriander
½ tsp paprika
200 g/7 oz canned chickpeas, drained and rinsed
1 egg, beaten
fine cornmeal or polenta, for coating
3–4 tbsp sesame seeds
sunflower oil, for frying

TOMATO SAUCE
1 tbsp olive oil
1 clove garlic, finely chopped
1 glass white wine, optional
400 g/14 oz passata
2 tsp tomato purée
½ tsp sugar
salt and freshly ground black pepper

❶ Place the rice in a saucepan and cover with the stock, stirring well. Bring to the boil, then reduce the heat and simmer, covered, for 15–20 minutes, or until the water has been absorbed and the rice is tender. Remove from the heat and leave the saucepan to sit, covered, for 5 minutes. Drain well and allow to cool for 30 minutes.

❷ To make the tomato sauce, heat the oil in a heavy-based saucepan and sauté the garlic for 1 minute, or until softened. Add the wine, if using, and cook over a high heat for a minute or so, until the alcohol has evaporated. Reduce the heat to medium, add the passata, tomato purée and sugar and cook for 15 minutes, or until the sauce has reduced and thickened. Season to taste and keep the sauce warm.

3 Meanwhile, make the rice balls. Heat the olive oil in a heavy-based frying pan. Add the onion and fry for 5–7 minutes, or until softened. Add the garlic and spices and cook for 1 minute, stirring. Stir in the chickpeas and the beaten egg.

4 Transfer the rice, chickpea, egg and onion mixture to a blender. Season to taste and process until thick and fairly smooth.

5 Cover a large plate with a layer of cornmeal and sprinkle over the sesame seeds. For each rice ball, take a walnut-sized amount of the rice mixture and form it into a ball, then roll it in the cornmeal and sesame seed mixture. Repeat until you have used all the rice mixture.

6 Heat enough oil to cover the base of a frying pan, then cook the rice balls for 4 minutes, turning occasionally, until crisp and golden. (You will have to cook the balls in batches.) Drain the rice balls on kitchen paper to mop up any excess oil.

7 To serve, divide the tomato sauce between 4 shallow bowls, then arrange the rice balls on top.

Banana Custard Scrunch

PREPARATION TIME *5 minutes* **COOKING TIME** *3 minutes*
FREEZING *unsuitable* **SERVES** *4 adults*

Layers of honey-coated oats, bananas and yogurt custard taste indulgent but couldn't be easier to make. Children love it when the scrunch is served in tall glasses with a long spoon.

INGREDIENTS
300 g/10½ oz thick natural yogurt
200 g/7 oz ready-made custard
70 g/2½ oz porridge oats
2 tbsp runny honey
2–3 bananas, sliced

❶ Mix together the yogurt and custard in a bowl.

❷ Put the oats in a dry frying pan and toast them for a minute. Add the honey and stir well to coat the oats. Cook for 2 minutes over a medium heat, stirring, until the oats become golden and slightly crisp at the edges.

❸ To serve, spoon the oat mixture, reserving a little to decorate, into the bottom of 4 glasses or ramekins. Arrange two-thirds of the banana over the oats, then top with the yogurt custard. Top with the reserved bananas and sprinkle with oats.

Strawberry & Vanilla Yogurt Ice

PREPARATION TIME *20 minutes* **FREEZING** *suitable*

SERVES *4 adults*

Yogurt adds a refreshing tang to this home-made fresh fruit ice, which can be scooped into small cones – the perfect size for toddlers of this age. Live yogurt has a beneficial effect on the digestive system and can help to fight off stomach upsets. As an added bonus, this ice is free from additives and stabilisers.

INGREDIENTS
350 g/12 oz thick live natural yogurt
200 g/7 oz mascarpone cheese
450 g/1 lb strawberries, hulled and sliced
1 tsp vanilla essence
6 tbsp runny honey

1. Whisk together the yogurt and mascarpone in a bowl. Pour into a shallow, freezer-proof container and freeze for 1 hour.

2. Purée the strawberries and vanilla essence in a blender until smooth, then mix with the honey.

3. Remove the semi-frozen yogurt mixture from the freezer and fold in the strawberry and honey mixture. Beat well.

4. Return the yogurt ice to the freezer and freeze for a further 2 hours. Remove from the freezer and beat again, then freeze until solid. Serve in scoops with fresh strawberries, if liked.

Baked Peach Crumbles

PREPARATION TIME *15 minutes* **COOKING TIME** *30 minutes*

FREEZING *suitable* **SERVES** *4 adults*

These individual crumbles are especially delicious with a good dollop of custard or ice cream. Plums and nectarines also work well.

INGREDIENTS

- 4 peaches, halved and stoned
- 40 g/1½ oz plain flour, sifted
- 2 tbsp butter, plus extra for greasing
- 2 tbsp porridge oats
- 3 tbsp light brown sugar

1. Preheat the oven to 180°C/350°F/Gas Mark 4.

2. Arrange the peach halves in the bottom of a small, lightly greased ovenproof dish.

3. Put the flour and butter in a bowl and rub together with your fingertips to form coarse breadcrumbs. Stir in the oats and sugar and mix well.

4. Sprinkle generous amounts of the crumble mixture over the peach halves. Bake for 25–30 minutes, or until the peaches are tender and the crumble mixture is slightly crisp and golden.

VARIATION

Add 1 tbsp of chopped mixed nuts and 1 tbsp finely chopped dried dates to the crumble mixture.

Mini Chocolate & Banana Muffins

PREPARATION TIME *10 minutes* **COOKING TIME** *15 minutes*

FREEZING *suitable* **MAKES** *24 small muffins*

These muffins are a good size for toddlers and are extremely delicious, especially when warm and the chocolate is still gooey.

1. Preheat the oven to 200°C/400°F/Gas Mark 6. Butter 2 x 12-hole small bun tins.

2. Sift together the flour, salt and baking powder in a large bowl. Add the sugar and chocolate to the flour mixture and then stir.

3. Place the milk, eggs, butter and yogurt in a separate bowl and whisk until combined. Add the egg mixture to the flour mixture, stirring until just combined, but don't overmix or it will result in heavy muffins.

4. Gently fold the mashed bananas into the mixture.

INGREDIENTS
140 g/5 oz plain flour
pinch of salt
1 tsp baking powder
140 g/5 oz light muscovado sugar
115 g/4 oz milk chocolate, broken into chunks
3 tbsp milk
2 eggs, beaten
140 g/5 oz unsalted butter, melted
3 tbsp low-fat natural yogurt
2 small bananas, mashed

5. Spoon the mixture into the greased bun tins and bake for 12–15 minutes, or until risen and slightly golden. Leave in the tin for 5 minutes, then turn out on to a wire rack to cool.

SECTION TWO

three to four years

Your toddler will by now be happily practising his or her eating skills, which can be a messy affair but nevertheless a crucial stage in a child's development. Accept and be prepared for the mess and try to resist the temptation to intervene too much. Alongside developing his or her own individuality, your 3 to 4-year-old will also become increasingly affected by outside influences, especially if he or she attends a playgroup or nursery. These factors can all play a part in determining food preferences.

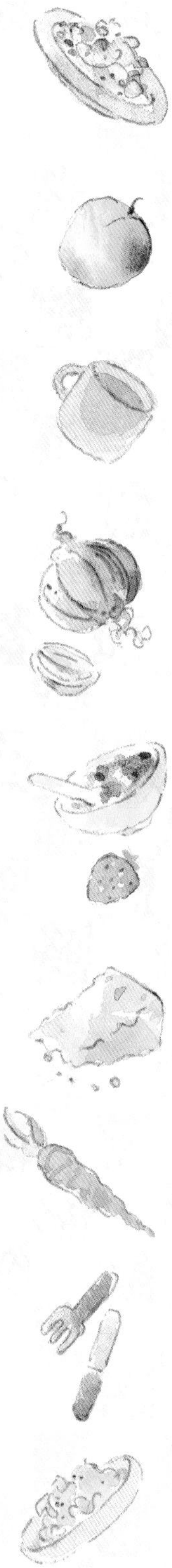

Nutritional Needs

The nutritional requirements of 3 to 4-year-olds are not that different from those of an 18-month-old. Although by this age the rate of growth has slowed down considerably, 3 to 4-year-olds are generally more active and their diets need to compensate for this increase in energy levels. High-energy foods still need to be included in your toddler's diet.

All small children require sufficient calories and a variety of foods (based on the major food groups mentioned on pages 6–9) to enable them to fuel high energy levels. They also need to be encouraged to enjoy the pleasures of eating and good food. This sounds simple in theory but good intentions can backfire in practice (see 'Coping with a fussy eater'). Do stick to your guns, however, and rest assured that by providing plenty of fresh, unprocessed foods you are doing the best for your child's health and development in the long term. Nutritionists suggest that a varied, healthy diet can help to curb the major diseases that plague us in the West later in life, and there is also evidence to show that a good diet can help to relieve the symptoms of asthma.

OUTSIDE INFLUENCES

Many 3 to 4-year-olds attend a playgroup or nursery and with this comes its own challenges. You may be fortunate to find an ideal establishment that serves a

BELOW *Your child's likes and dislikes may be influenced by the nursery food that they are offered.*

variety of freshly prepared, nutritious lunches, snacks and healthy drinks. Realistically, food standards tend to vary and it can be awkward for parents to ask for changes without appearing difficult and demanding. Many nurseries are open to parents providing their own drinks, snacks and packed lunches and this may be a welcome option. Alternatively, take the softly-softly approach, arming yourself with relevant information, articles and books. Often a lack of knowledge is to blame for poor food quality and all that is needed is a little encouragement.

EATING OUT

It can be a challenge to find a restaurant that not only welcomes children with open arms but also provides decent healthy food. Most children's menus offer the usual repertoire of fish fingers and chips, burger and chips, and sausage and chips, followed by poor-quality ice cream and jelly. There is also the further lure of a free gift! Consequently, all your good intentions fly out of the window.

Most children love the novelty of eating out and, from experience, the better quality pizza chains, Italian, Indian and Chinese restaurants offer the best choice and are often more welcoming to families with young children. Alternatively, choose a starter from the main menu or ask for a separate plate and share your meal. Sometimes the chef may provide a small child-sized portion of a main course.

Eating out can be a hit-or-miss affair, and it is best to pick a time when your little one is not very tired, or choose a restaurant that appears too formal, where it may be difficult to relax. To prevent occasional boredom, take along pens and paper or a small toy to keep your child entertained.

ABOVE *Eating out with a young child is a valuable experience and can be enjoyed by the whole family.*

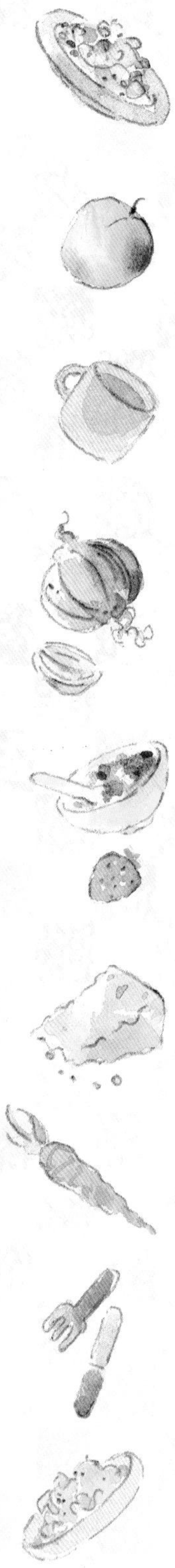

Coping With a Fussy Eater

All toddlers go through stages of picky eating and their appetites can be equally unpredictable. However frustrating this may be, try not to let this trouble you. There are plenty of stories of toddlers surviving on nothing but toast and jam for some unimaginable amount of time – remarkably, most don't seem to suffer adverse effects.

How do you encourage your child to eat what you want him or her to, and what do you do if he or she refuses to eat at all? There are no easy answers, but the following guidelines should help you cope more easily with those challenging times:

• Don't force your child to eat. Conflict and tension serve only to make the situation worse and may lead to your child using mealtimes as a way of seeking attention. Children are remarkably clever at picking up on the anxieties of their parents and may well pick up on your own insecurities about food. Instead, try to gently coax or encourage your child to try a little bit of what you have prepared. I've found that my daughter will happily eat a meal once I've encouraged her to try 'just a mouthful'.

• If your gentle coaxing doesn't work, remove the food without making a fuss, but don't offer an alternative dish, however hard this may be. I know, speaking as someone who has prepared numerous alternatives when my daughter has refused to eat, that this is a losing battle. Your child is unlikely to starve and it's important that they learn to eat what's on offer, rather than expect endless alternatives.

• Don't overload your child's plate. Small amounts of food tend to be more acceptable.

• Praise and encourage your child as much as possible, even if they eat only a mouthful.

• Make eating fun. Picnics, even if it's only a cloth arranged on the kitchen floor, games, or basing a meal on a theme, such as a

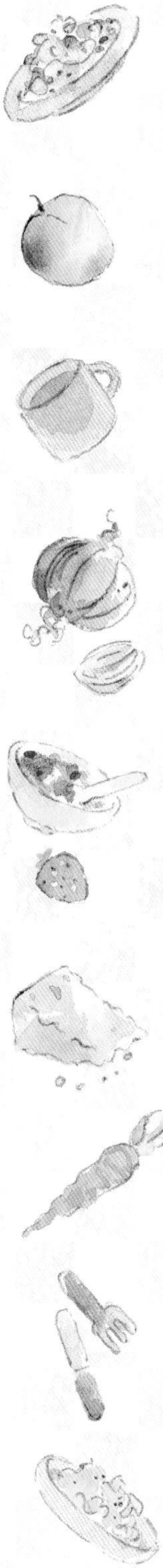

favourite cartoon character, book or season, can be a real success.

ABOVE *Presenting small portions of food to your toddler is less off-putting and seems more manageable.*

• Try to ignore poor eating habits and complaints such as 'yuck', however hard this may be.

• Ask a friend of your child's, who you know to be a good eater, to come to tea. Children often learn by example and may be encouraged to eat by their peers. Beware, this can sometimes backfire – my daughter hasn't eaten peas since a friend said she disliked them!

• Don't fall into the trap of bribing your child with a pudding, and then giving it even if the main meal remains uneaten. This will only help to discourage good eating habits.

• Compromise is sometimes the only way to get your child to eat certain things. Combine foods that you know your child likes with others that are untried or previously rejected.

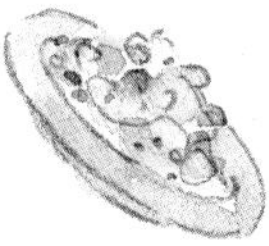

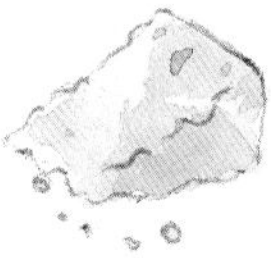
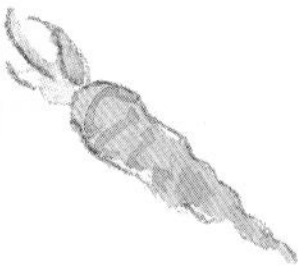

MEAL PLANNER 2

3-4 YEARS	BREAKFAST	LUNCH
Day 1	Diced bacon & grilled tomatoes Toast, yogurt	Pasta bolognese, broccoli Fruit salad
Day 2	Porridge, fruit, toast	Frittata, coleslaw Baked apple and custard
Day 3	Cereal/muesli, muffin	Tomato & lentil soup Garlic bread with cheese Chocolate muffin
Day 4	Poached egg & beans Toast Yogurt	Higgledy-piggledy pie with potatoes and vegetables Ice cream sundae
Day 5	Cereal, toast	Starfish pie with French beans Chocolate bread pudding
Day 6	Pancake with stewed apple Yogurt	Pork & apple casserole Potatoes & vegetables Baked peach crumbles
Day 7	Cheese scrambled eggs on toast Fruit	Sausage hot pot Vegetables Sandcastle cakes

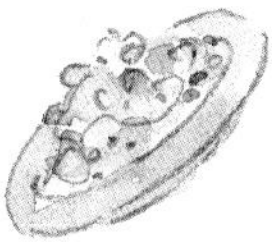

TEA	SUPPER
Paella Ice cream sundae	Guacamole with tortilla pitta bread Vegetable sticks Fruit & milky drink
Chinese noodles Banana custard scrunch	Tortilla parcel Fruit & milky drink
Golden fish fingers & potato wedges with peas Strawberry yogurt ice	Sardines on toast Fruit & milky drink
Chicken sticks, coleslaw Baked potato Fromage frais & fruit	Cheese on toast Fruit & milky drink
Rice balls with tomato sauce, vegetables Yogurt	Sandwich Fruit & milky drink
Smoked salmon & broccoli pasta Flapjack	Houmus/cheese tortilla Vegetable sticks Fruit & milky drink
Baked potato with pesto & cheese Pancake with hot maple bananas	Raisin & pecan muffins Fruit & milky drink

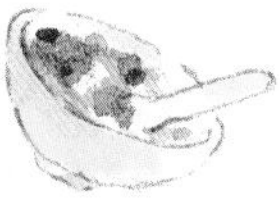
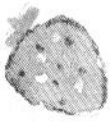

Creamy Tomato & Lentil Soup

PREPARATION TIME *10 minutes* **COOKING TIME** *45 minutes*

FREEZING *suitable* **SERVES** *4 adults*

Remarkably, children who turn their noses up at vegetables will happily eat them when liquidised into a soup. Most toddlers love tomato soup, and this one is free from the additives often found in manufactured alternatives. The lentils add extra goodness and substance, but they can be swapped for beans or cooked rice. I usually serve this soup with mini cheese toasts, although croûtons, garlic bread or a hunk of crusty bread are just as good.

INGREDIENTS

55 g/2 oz split red lentils, rinsed

1 tbsp olive oil

1 onion, chopped

1 carrot, peeled and finely chopped

1 celery stick, chopped

500 g/1 lb 2 oz carton creamed tomatoes

600 ml/1 pint vegetable stock

cream or natural yogurt, to serve (optional)

salt and freshly ground black pepper

CHEESE TOASTS

8 slices French bread

butter, for spreading

55 g/2 oz Gruyère or mature Cheddar cheese, grated

½ tsp dried oregano

1. Place the lentils in a saucepan, cover with water and bring to the boil. Reduce the heat and simmer, half covered, for 25 minutes, or until tender. Drain the lentils well and set them aside.

2. While the lentils are cooking, make the soup. Heat the oil in a heavy-based saucepan. Add the onion, cover the pan and sweat for 10 minutes, or until softened. Add the carrot and celery and sweat for a further 2 minutes, stirring occasionally to prevent the vegetables sticking to the bottom of the pan and burning.

3. Add the creamed tomatoes and stock and bring to the boil. Reduce the heat and simmer, half covered, for 25 minutes, or until the vegetables are tender and the liquid has reduced and thickened. Add the lentils to the pan.

4. Carefully pour the mixture into a blender and blend until smooth and creamy. Return the soup to the pan, season to taste and heat through if necessary. Swirl a spoonful of cream, if using, over the soup and serve.

5. For the cheese toasts, preheat the grill to high. Lightly toast the French bread on one side. Butter the untoasted side and sprinkle with the Gruyère cheese and oregano. Grill until golden.

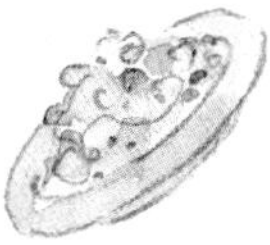

Golden Fish Fingers with Sweet Potato Wedges

PREPARATION TIME *15 minutes* **COOKING TIME** *35 minutes*

FREEZING *suitable* **MAKES** *8–10 fingers*

If making your own fish fingers sounds like too much effort, this simple, quick version may change your mind, and you can also guarantee the quality of the ingredients used. The cod fillets are covered in a crisp, golden crumb, made from fresh breadcrumbs, and I like to serve them with these sweet potato wedges.

❶ Preheat the oven to 200°C/400°F/Gas Mark 6.

❷ Dry the sweet potato wedges on a clean tea towel. Place the oil in a roasting tin and heat for a few minutes in the oven. Arrange the potatoes in the tin and bake for 30–35 minutes, turning them halfway through, until tender and golden.

❸ Meanwhile, cut the cod into strips, about 2 cm/¾ in wide.

❹ Season the flour and add the paprika. Roll the cod strips in the seasoned flour until coated, shaking off any excess, then dip them in the beaten egg. Roll the cod strips in the breadcrumbs until evenly coated.

❺ Heat enough oil to cover the base of a large, non-stick frying pan. Carefully arrange the fish fingers in the pan – you may have to cook them in batches – and fry them for 3–4 minutes on each side, or until crisp and golden. Drain on kitchen paper before serving, if necessary.

❻ Serve the fish fingers with the sweet potato wedges and peas.

INGREDIENTS

280 g/10 oz thick cod fillets, skin and bones removed

flour, for dusting

1 tsp paprika

1 egg, beaten

fresh breadcrumbs or fine cornmeal, for coating

sunflower oil, for frying

salt and freshly ground black pepper

SWEET POTATO WEDGES

450 g/1 lb sweet potatoes, scrubbed and cut into wedges

1 tbsp olive oil

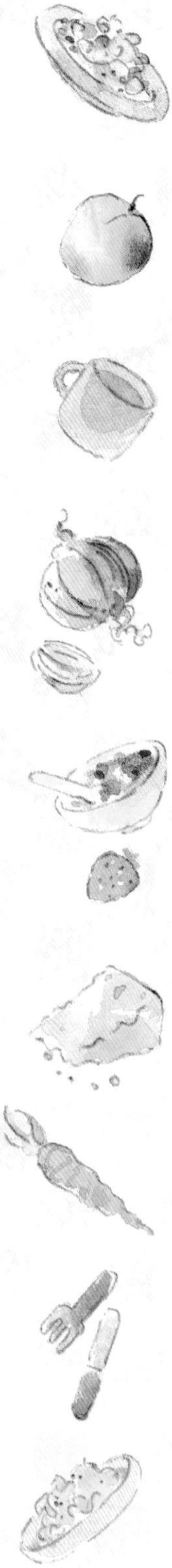

Surf 'n' Turf Paella

PREPARATION TIME *15 minutes* **COOKING TIME** *30 minutes*

FREEZING *suitable* **SERVES** *2–3 adults*

This golden rice dish is infused with saffron, but you can use turmeric instead, which gives a similar sunshine colour. Paella rice is perfect for young children as it has a tender, melt-in-the-mouth texture when cooked.

❶ Heat the oil in a large heavy-based sauté pan (with a lid). Add the onion and fry for 5 minutes, or until softened. Add the chicken breast, pepper and garlic and sauté for 5 minutes over a medium heat, stirring frequently to prevent the mixture sticking.

➋ Add the tomato, tomato purée, saffron and stock to the pan. Stir in the rice and bring to the boil, then reduce the heat. Simmer the rice, covered, for 15 minutes, or until the rice is tender.

➌ Add the peas, prawns and seasoning and cook for a further 2–3 minutes, or until the prawns have heated through.

INGREDIENTS

2 tbsp olive oil

1 onion, diced

2 skinless chicken breasts, sliced

1 small red pepper, seeded and diced

2 cloves garlic, chopped

1 tomato, seeded and chopped

1 tbsp tomato purée

pinch of saffron

600 ml/1 pint hot chicken or vegetable stock

175 g/6 oz paella rice

55 g/2 oz frozen peas

115 g/4 oz cooked prawns, defrosted if frozen

salt and freshly ground black pepper

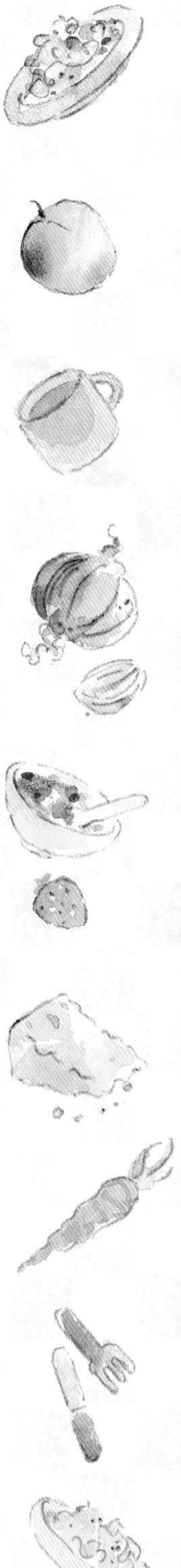

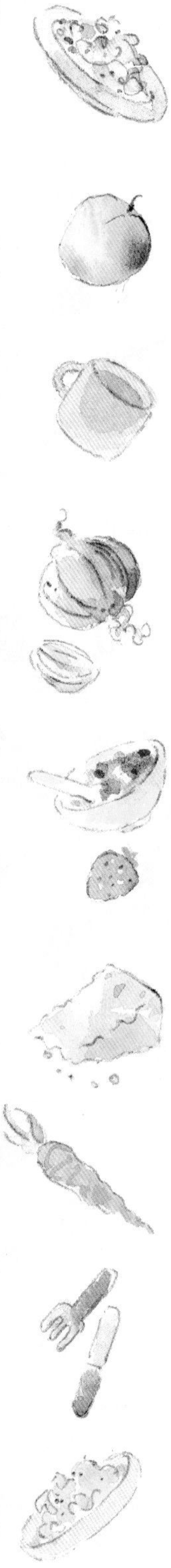

Pasta Bolognese

PREPARATION TIME *10 minutes* **COOKING TIME** *30 minutes*

FREEZING *suitable* **SERVES** *4 adults*

Spaghetti is a real favourite with toddlers, who love the slurping and the accompanying mess – so be prepared! Vegetarians can opt for soya mince or Quorn instead of meat. Use good-quality mince if opting for the meat-eater's version.

❶ Heat the oil in a heavy-based, non-stick saucepan. Add the onion and sauté, half covered, for 5 minutes, or until softened. Add the garlic, carrot and mushrooms, if using, and sauté for a further 3 minutes, stirring occasionally.

INGREDIENTS

350 g/12 oz spaghetti or pasta of your choice

BOLOGNESE SAUCE

2 tbsp olive oil

1 onion, finely chopped

2 cloves garlic, finely chopped

1 carrot, peeled and finely chopped

85 g/3 oz mushrooms, peeled and sliced or chopped (optional)

1 tsp dried oregano

½ tsp dried thyme

1 bay leaf

280 g/10 oz lean mince

1 glass white wine (optional)

300 ml/10 fl oz stock

300 ml/10 fl oz passata

salt and freshly ground black pepper

2 Add the herbs and mince to the pan and cook until the meat has browned, stirring regularly.

3 Add the wine, if using, and cook over a high heat until the alcohol has evaporated, then add the stock and passata. Reduce the heat, season to taste and cook over a low–medium heat, half covered, for 15–20 minutes, or until the sauce has reduced and thickened. Remove the bay leaf.

4 Meanwhile, cook the pasta according to the instructions on the packet, until the pasta is tender. Drain well and mix together the pasta and sauce until the pasta is well coated.

Bacon, Pea & Potato Frittata

PREPARATION TIME *15 minutes* **COOKING TIME** *20 minutes*

FREEZING *unsuitable* **SERVES** *3–4 adults*

This frittata is similar to the Spanish tortilla. Serve it cut into wedges or fingers, with crusty bread and green vegetables or a salad. This is a good food for small fingers to handle.

1 Preheat the grill to high. Grill the bacon until crisp. Allow to cool slightly, then cut into small pieces and set aside.

2 Heat the oil in a large heavy-based, ovenproof frying pan, add the onion and sauté for 5 minutes, or until softened and tender stirring occasionally.

INGREDIENTS

2–3 slices good-quality bacon

1½ tbsp olive oil

1 small onion, finely chopped

350 g/12 oz new potatoes, cooked, halved or quartered, if large

55 g/2 oz frozen petit pois

6 free range eggs, lightly beaten

salt and freshly ground black pepper

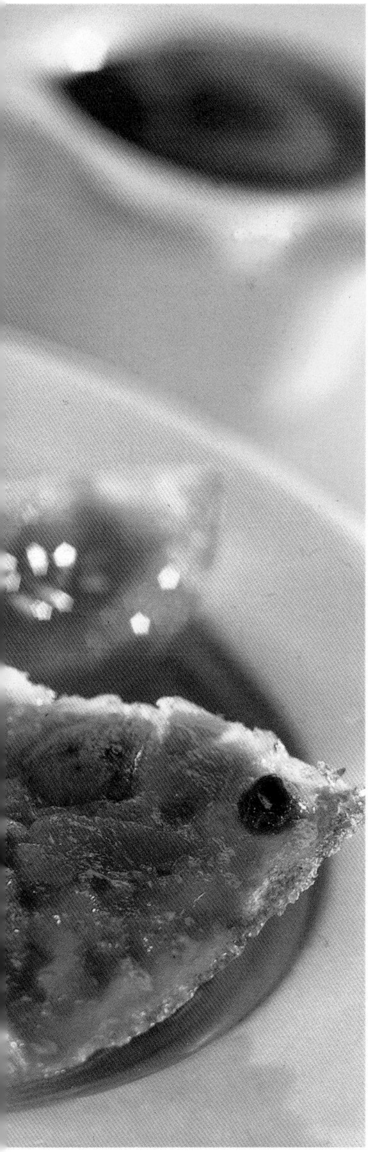

2 Add the potatoes and cook for a further 5 minutes, or until golden, stirring to prevent them sticking to the pan. Add the bacon pieces and peas, and spread the mixture evenly over the base of the pan.

3 Reheat the grill to high. Season the beaten eggs, then pour them carefully over the onion and potato mixture. Cook over a moderate heat for 5–6 minutes, or until the eggs are just set and the base of the frittata is lightly golden brown.

4 Place the pan under the grill and cook the top for 3 minutes, or until set and lightly golden. Serve the frittata warm or cold, cut into wedges or fingers.

Chinese Noodles

PREPARATION TIME *10 minutes, plus 1 hour marinating*
COOKING TIME *20 minutes* **FREEZING** *unsuitable* **SERVES** *4 adults*

Toddlers seem to love noodles as much as pasta and this stir-fry is no exception. I've chosen brightly coloured vegetables for maximum appeal, but experiment with different types. Whatever you choose, they are at their best when still slightly crunchy.

❶ Mix together the ingredients for the marinade in a shallow dish. Add the tofu and spoon the marinade over. Refrigerate for 1 hour to marinate, turning the tofu occasionally to allow the flavours to infuse.

❷ Preheat the oven to 200°C/400°F/Gas Mark 6. Using a slotted spoon, remove the tofu from the marinade and reserve the liquid. Arrange the tofu on a baking sheet and roast for 20 minutes, turning occasionally,

INGREDIENTS

250 g/9 oz medium egg noodles

250 g pack of tofu, cubed

1 tbsp peanut or vegetable oil

1 red pepper, seeded and sliced

225 g/8 oz broccoli florets

175 g/6 oz baby sweetcorn, halved lengthways

2–3 tbsp water

2 spring onions, finely sliced

1 tbsp sesame seeds, toasted (optional)

MARINADE

1 clove garlic, finely chopped

2.5-cm/1-in piece fresh root ginger, peeled and grated

1 tsp sesame oil

1 tbsp runny honey

2 tbsp dark soy sauce

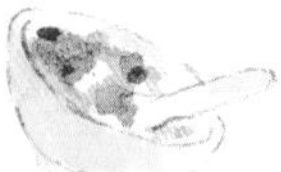

until the tofu pieces are golden and crisp on all sides.

❸ Meanwhile, cook the noodles in plenty of salted boiling water according to the instructions on the packet, until the noodles are tender, then drain. Rinse the noodles under cold running water and drain again.

❹ Heat a wok or heavy-based frying pan, then add the oil. Add the pepper, broccoli and sweetcorn and stir-fry, tossing and stirring continuously, over a medium-high heat for 5–8 minutes, or until the vegetables have softened. Add the water and continue to stir-fry until the vegetables are just tender but remain slightly crunchy.

❺ Stir in the marinade, noodles, tofu and spring onions, and stir-fry until heated through, tossing to coat them in the liquid.

❻ Serve sprinkled with sesame seeds, if using.

Winter Sausage Hot Pot

PREPARATION TIME *15 minutes* **COOKING TIME** *45 minutes*
FREEZING *suitable* **SERVES** *4 adults*

A satisfying, warming stew, which has a savoury scone topping and can be made with either pork or vegetarian sausages. The alcohol in the wine will evaporate during cooking.

❶ Preheat the grill to high. Grill the sausages, turning them occasionally, until they are cooked and golden. Set aside.

❷ Preheat the oven to 200°C/400°F/Gas Mark 6.

❸ Meanwhile, heat the oil in a heavy-based saucepan and sauté the onion, covered, for 5 minutes, or until softened. Add the garlic, celery, pepper, ourgettes and herbs and sauté, covered, for a further 5 minutes.

❹ Add the wine, if using, and cook over a medium-high heat for a few minutes until the alcohol has evaporated. If using

the wine, add the smaller amount of stock; if not, opt for the greater quantity. Reduce the heat to medium, stir and add the passata and sugar. Stir again and cook for 10 minutes, or until the sauce has reduced and begins to thicken.

❺ Slice the cooked sausages and add them to the sauce with the beans. Stir and spoon the mixture into a casserole dish.

❻ To make the scone topping, place the flour, salt and baking powder into a bowl and mix. Add the margarine and rub with your fingertips until the mixture forms breadcrumbs.

❼ Gradually stir in the milk using a palette knife and form the mixture into a dough with your floured hands. Knead lightly on a floured work surface until smooth. Take walnut-sized pieces of the dough and roll them into balls. Flatten them and arrange them in a circle on the top.

❽ Brush the top of the scones with milk and bake for 20 minutes, or until the scones have risen and are golden.

INGREDIENTS

6 pork or vegetarian sausages
1 tbsp olive oil
1 onion, chopped
1 clove garlic, chopped
1 celery stick, finely chopped
1 red pepper, seeded and diced
2 courgettes, sliced
2 tsp chopped fresh rosemary
1 tsp thyme
1 bay leaf
1 glass of white wine (optional)
150–300 ml/5–10 fl oz vegetable stock
300 ml/10 fl oz passata
½ tsp sugar
400-g/14-oz can borlotti beans, drained and rinsed

SCONE TOPPING

175 g/6 oz self-raising flour, sifted
½ tsp salt
1 heaped tsp baking powder
3 tbsp butter or margarine
50–80 ml/2–3 fl oz milk, plus extra for glazing

Higgledy-Piggledy Pie

PREPARATION TIME *20 minutes, plus 30 minutes resting*
COOKING TIME *55 minutes* **FREEZING** *suitable* **SERVES** *4 adults*

This free-form pie encases a rich tomato, aubergine and kidney bean filling. If your pastry cracks, just patch it up – it adds to the pie's rustic charm. The pastry is enriched with Parmesan cheese, but this can be omitted if desired.

❶ Preheat the oven to 220°C/425°F/Gas Mark 7. For the pastry, rub the plain and wholemeal flours, salt and butter together until the mixture resembles fine breadcrumbs, then stir in the Parmesan cheese.

❷ Add enough cold water to form a dough, then turn out the dough on to a lightly floured work surface and knead lightly to form a smooth and elastic dough. Wrap in clingfilm and chill for 30 minutes.

INGREDIENTS

450 g/1 lb aubergine, cubed
1 red pepper, seeded and diced
2 tbsp olive oil
1 onion, finely chopped
1 courgette, sliced
2 cloves garlic, crushed
1 tsp dried oregano
200 g/7 oz canned red kidney beans, drained and rinsed
salt and freshly ground black pepper
375 g/13 oz chopped tomatoes
2 tbsp semolina
55 g/2 oz Cheddar cheese, grated
1 egg, beaten, to glaze

PASTRY

115 g/4 oz plain flour
115 g/4 oz wholemeal flour
115 g/4 oz butter or vegetable margarine
55 g/2 oz Parmesan cheese, finely grated

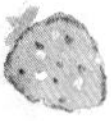

❸ To make the filling, sprinkle the aubergine with salt and leave for 30 minutes to remove any bitter juices. Rinse and pat dry with kitchen paper.

❹ Heat the oil in a large heavy-based frying pan. Fry the onions for 5 minutes, or until softened, stirring occasionally. Add the pepper and aubergine and fry for 5 minutes, or until tender, then add the courgette, garlic and oregano. Cook for a further 5 minutes. Add the kidney beans, seasoning and chopped tomatoes. Cook for 8 minutes, or until the sauce has reduced, then cool.

❺ Divide the pastry into four pieces and roll out on a lightly floured work surface to form equal-sized rounds. Place on a lightly greased baking sheet. Brush with a little of the beaten egg and sprinkle over the semolina, leaving a 4-cm/1½-in border. Spoon over the filling, leaving a border, and sprinkle with the Cheddar cheese.

❻ Gather up the edges of the pastry to partly cover the filling – the pie should remain open in the middle. Brush with the remaining egg and bake for 25–30 minutes, or until the pastry is golden.

Tortilla Parcels

PREPARATION TIME *5 minutes* **COOKING TIME** *2 minutes*
FREEZING *unsuitable* **MAKES** *2 parcels*

Soft, floury tortillas make a perfect snack or light lunch. These are filled with tuna, mozzarella cheese and diced tomato, but you could vary the filling according to likes and dislikes. Guacamole or houmus are also popular with children.

INGREDIENTS

4 slices of mozzarella cheese, drained and dried with kitchen paper

2 tbsp canned tuna in oil, drained and mashed

1 small tomato, seeded and diced

1 soft tortilla

salt and freshly ground black pepper

❶ Place the mozzarella cheese, tuna, tomato and seasoning along the centre of the tortilla. Fold in the sides, then the ends of the tortilla to encase the filling.

❷ Place the parcel, seam-side down, in a dry, non-stick frying pan and gently warm over a low-medium heat for 2 minutes, turning once, until the tortilla is lightly golden and the filling is warmed through. Cut the tortilla in half and serve immediately.

Ice Cream Strawberry Sundae

PREPARATION TIME *10 minutes* **COOKING TIME** *12 minutes*

FREEZING *sauce can be frozen* **SERVES** *4*

This sumptuous dessert is a real treat, and is enjoyed by adults and children alike! Strawberries are particularly popular with toddlers, and they are sweet enough not to need too much extra sugar. Be sure to use good-quality dairy ice cream.

❶ To make the sauce, process the strawberries with the orange juice in a blender until smooth. Transfer the mixture to a saucepan and add the sugar. Cook over a medium heat for 10–12 minutes, or until thickened. Leave to cool.

INGREDIENTS

8 scoops of good-quality vanilla ice cream

25 g/1 oz chopped mixed nuts, lightly toasted in a dry frying pan

grated chocolate and marshmallows, to serve

STRAWBERRY SAUCE

250 g/9 oz strawberries, hulled and halved

2 tbsp freshly squeezed orange juice

2 tbsp caster sugar

❷ To serve, place a spoonful of the strawberry sauce in the bottom of a tall glass. Add two scoops of ice cream and another spoonful of fruit sauce. Sprinkle with the nuts and chocolate. Arrange the marshmallows on top. Repeat for four sundaes.

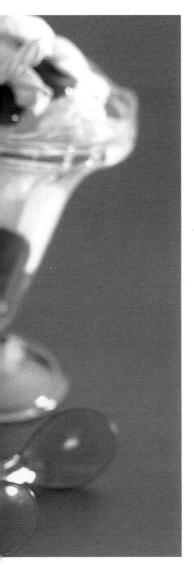

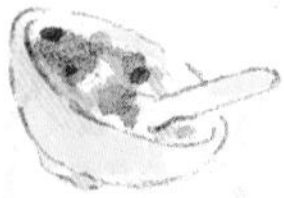

VARIATION

Replace the strawberry sauce with a rich chocolate sauce. Melt 100 g/3½ oz of good-quality milk chocolate in a bowl, placed over a pan of simmering water. (Make sure the bowl does not touch the water.) Stir very occasionally until melted. Heat 2 tbsp milk, 50 ml/2 fl oz double cream and 2 tbsp caster sugar in a small saucepan and bring to the boil. Gently pour the mixture onto the melted chocolate and whisk until combined and smooth. Serve warm.

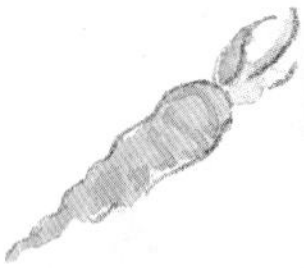

Fruity Chocolate Bread Pudding

PREPARATION TIME *15 minutes* **COOKING TIME** *35 minutes*

FREEZING *suitable* **SERVES** *4 adults*

A rich, comforting pudding that just melts in the mouth. It is made with fruit bread, but ordinary sliced bread, muffins, brioche or panettone work just as well. Toddlers love it with custard.

1. Preheat the oven to 200°C/400°F/Gas Mark 6. Butter a 25 x 20-cm/10 x 8-in baking dish. Arrange half the fruit bread in the dish in a single layer.

2. Spread the fruit bread with the chocolate spread. Arrange another layer of fruit bread over the chocolate bread, making sure that it lies flat.

3 Gently heat the milk and vanilla essence in a saucepan, until it just reaches boiling point. Remove from the heat and whisk in the egg and maple syrup, mixing well.

4 Pour the egg mixture over the fruit, lightly pressing down the bread so it is submerged. Leave to soak for 10 minutes.

5 Bake for 25–30 minutes, or until set and golden. To serve, cut into 4 portions and sprinkle the top of the pudding with ground cinnamon.

INGREDIENTS

275 g/9½ oz sliced fruit bread, crusts removed

6 tbsp good-quality chocolate spread

300 ml/10 fl oz milk

½ tsp vanilla essence

1 large free-range egg, beaten

1 tbsp maple syrup

ground cinnamon, for decorating

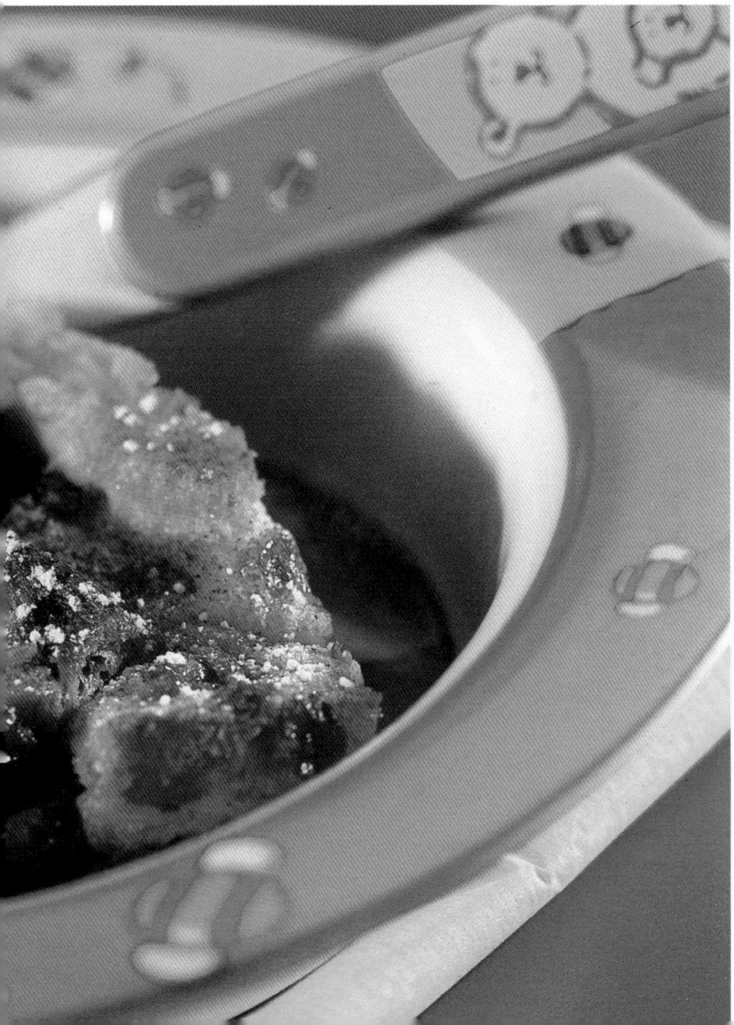

Buttermilk Pancakes with Hot Maple Bananas

PREPARATION TIME *5 minutes* **COOKING TIME** *5 minutes*

FREEZING *pancakes suitable* **SERVES** *4 adults*

A simple and very quick pudding-cum-breakfast that nevertheless tastes delicious. Serve the pancakes with a spoonful of fromage frais, natural yogurt or vanilla ice cream.

INGREDIENTS

3 tbsp unsalted butter

4 bananas, thickly sliced diagonally

6 tbsp maple syrup

1 tbsp flaked almonds, toasted (optional)

PANCAKES

140 g/5 oz plain flour, sifted

pinch of salt

2 tbsp caster sugar

1 tsp baking powder

1 egg, beaten

300 ml/10 fl oz carton buttermilk

25 g/1 oz butter, melted

sunflower oil, for frying

❶ To make the pancakes, place the flour, salt, sugar and baking powder in a large bowl and mix everything together well.

❷ Mix together the beaten egg, buttermilk and melted butter, then add it to the flour mixture and beat well to remove any lumps. (This makes a thick batter.)

❸ Heat a teaspoon of the oil in a heavy-based frying pan. Place heaped tablespoons of the batter in the pan and flatten with the back of a spoon. Cook for 3 minutes, or until set and golden, then turn over and cook the other side of the pancake for 2 minutes. Cover with foil and keep warm in an ovenproof dish placed in a preheated oven. Make the remaining pancakes.

❹ Melt the butter in a heavy-based frying pan. Add the bananas and cook for 1 minute over a medium heat, turning once to coat them in the butter.

❺ Add the maple syrup and cook the bananas for 1–2 minutes. To serve, spoon the bananas and syrup over the pancakes.

Sandcastle Cakes

PREPARATION TIME *10 minutes* **COOKING TIME** *20 minutes*

FREEZING *unsuitable* **MAKES** *4 cakes*

These fun, decorated sponge cakes are great for parties or a special teatime treat when your children have been extra good! Top the cakes with home-made flags with each child's name on it for an added fun factor.

INGREDIENTS

115 g/4 oz self-raising flour

115 g/4 oz caster sugar

115 g/4 oz butter or margarine, plus extra for greasing

2 eggs

3 tbsp strawberry jam

silver balls and hundreds and thousands, to decorate

1. Preheat the oven to 180°C/350°F/Gas Mark 4. Lightly grease 4 dariole moulds and line the base with a circle of greaseproof paper.

2. Sift the flour into a large mixing bowl. Add the sugar, butter and eggs and beat together until smooth and creamy.

3. Divide the mixture between the moulds, filling them three-quarters full. Place on a baking sheet and cook for 20 minutes, or until risen and golden. Leave for 5 minutes, then turn out to cool.

4. Trim the base of each cake so they stand up. Heat the jam in a saucepan until runny, then brush it over the top and sides of the cakes. Sprinkle or roll the cakes in the hundreds and thousands and decorate with the silver balls.

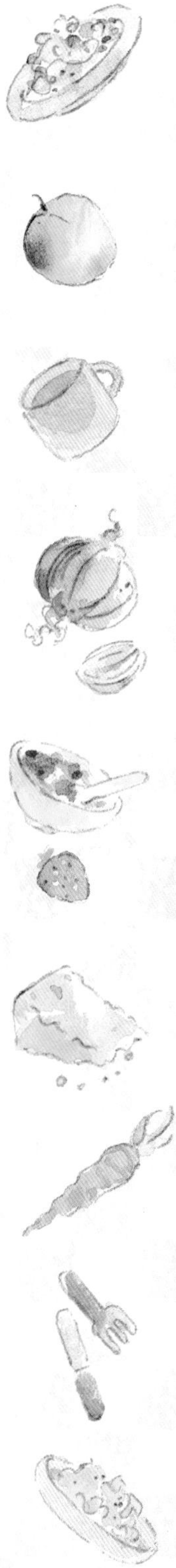

SECTION THREE

four plus

By this stage, your little one will be making the transition from toddler to young child, and with this comes an increasing independence and free spirit. It is important to allow your child's personality, sense of humour and sense of self to flourish, without knocking his or her confidence if he or she sometimes goes awry. This is especially important at mealtimes, when guidance, gentle persuasion and plenty of patience are vital.

Nutritional Needs

For many young children, their fourth year heralds the start of full-time education. School presents its own challenges and it can be a time when good intentions and eating habits fall by the wayside. However, a nutritious, varied diet is an important as ever – sustaining and boosting energy levels, concentration and, some experts even say, brain power.

Many children do not eat breakfast before they go to school or simply rely on a bag of crisps or a chocolate bar to fight off hunger pangs until lunchtime. Many nutritionists believe that breakfast is the most important meal of the day, replenishing nutrients and energy stocks depleted overnight. High-carbohydrate foods such as low-sugar breakfast cereals, bread and beans provide sustained energy and help to keep blood sugar levels on an even keel. Recent research suggests that children who eat a carbohydrate-based breakfast are likely to perform better at school.

School lunches vary in quality and choice depending on where you live, with some councils abolishing them altogether. A packed lunch may be the only way you can ensure that your child is getting nutritious food – that's as long as it's eaten! Turn to page 77 for some ideas. At this age, tea or supper may become the main meal of the day. Even if your child has a cooked school lunch, it's advisable to give him or her a decent meal in the afternoon or evening to ensure that he or she is getting a sufficient range of nutrients. Now your child is older, it may be feasible to eat communal meals. Eating together encourages children to try a wider variety of food as well as to enjoy the social aspect of sharing mealtimes.

JUNK FOODS

There are very few completely 'bad' foods, but there are many which are best avoided – those containing E numbers and other additives, artificial colourings, sweeteners, hydrogenated and saturated fat, as well as excessively sugary and salty foods. Poor-quality foods, including cheap biscuits, cakes, processed meats and cheeses, pies, sugary fizzy drinks and

packet desserts are just some of the foods that fall into this category. If finances allow, it is really worth buying healthier alternatives, which are usually made with superior ingredients.

We all buy convenience foods, but do try to opt for fish fingers containing the highest percentage of fish, sausages and pies with a high meat content, jam with a high fruit content and biscuits, cakes and cereals that are lower in sugar than others. Better still, it really is worth taking the time to make your own versions and ensure that fruit or vegetables play an important part.

• To make healthier chips: cut potatoes into wedges, retaining the skin, then brush with olive oil and bake in the oven. Good source of vitamin C and fibre.

ABOVE *A good breakfast before a day at school is vital to keep energy levels high, and stops your child snacking.*

• Top a pizza base with home-made tomato sauce, grated cheese and vegetables. Good source of vitamin C, beta-carotene and calcium.

• Use lean meat and grated vegetables to make home-made burgers. Combine mashed beans and grated vegetables to make a vegetarian alternative. Brush the burgers with oil and grill. Good source of iron, vitamins C and B.

• Make a healthier version of a 'knickerbocker glory' with natural yogurt or good-quality ice cream, fresh fruit purée and chopped toasted nuts. Pile high in a glass. A good source of vitamins B, C and calcium.

MEAL PLANNER 3

4+ YEARS	BREAKFAST	LUNCH
Day 1	Porridge and dried apricots Toast	Noodle soup with chicken/ tofu/prawns, fromage frais OR packed/school lunch
Day 2	Boiled egg, toast, banana	Chicken, apple & nut salad, bread Baked apple & custard OR packed/school lunch
Day 3	Cereal, toasted fruit bread	Chinese omelette roll, yogurt OR packed/school lunch
Day 4	Toasted bacon and tomato sandwich, yogurt	Bean & pasta soup Tortilla parcel Strawberry & vanilla ice OR packed/school lunch
Day 5	Cereal, toast, melon	Smoked salmon & broccoli pasta Fresh fruit sticks OR packed/school lunch
Day 6	Bubble & squeak cakes Grilled tomatoes Fresh orange juice	Rice balls in tomato sauce Chicken fingers Ice cream sundae
Day 7	Scrambled egg Kipper & toast	Christmas pie Roast potatoes & vegetables Little Jack Horner pudding

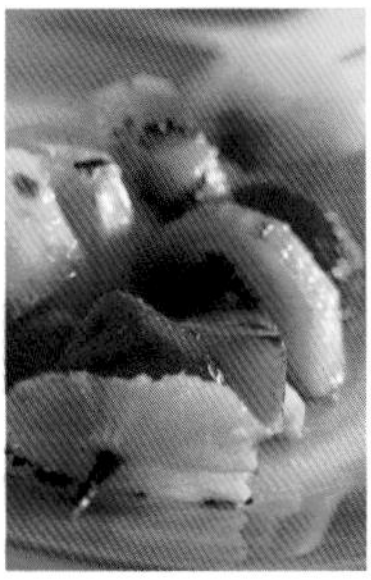

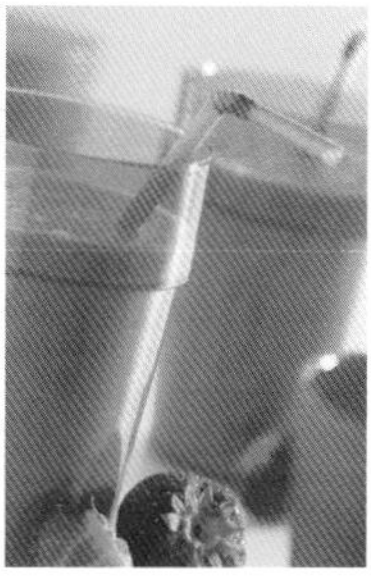

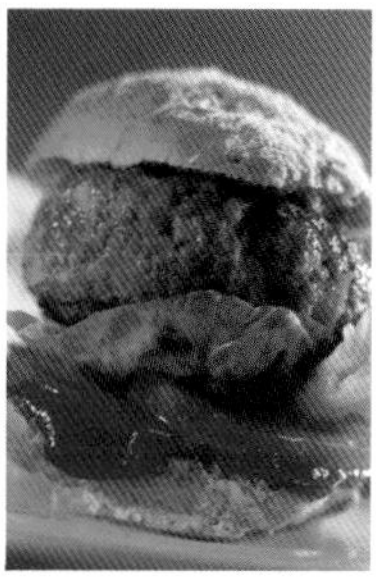

TEA	SUPPER
Sunny rice, green vegetables Pancakes with maple bananas	Sandwich, fruit Milky drink
Green giant pasta Garlic bread Sponge sandcastles	Muffin/scone Fruit Milky drink
Honey salmon kebabs, rice and vegetables Passion cake squares	Crackers & cheese Apple & grapes Milky drink
Mini burger & bun Sweet potato wedges Grated carrot Baked peach crumbles	Sardines on toast Fruit Milky drink
Sausage hot pot, vegetables Fromage frais	Gingerbread person Fruit Milky drink
Pork & apple casserole Potatoes & vegetables Chocolate bread pudding	Malt loaf Fruit Milky drink
Tomato & lentil soup Pizza fingers Banana custard scrunch	Sandwich Fruit Milky drink

Lunchbox Ideas

Many of us get stuck in a rut when it comes to providing interesting and varied lunchboxes everyday – it's all too easy to stick to the usual sandwich, crisps, yogurt and apple. Time is also at a premium in the morning, when preparing a lunchbox has to be juggled with breakfast, getting dressed and the school run. The following ideas will hopefully inspire and most can be prepared ahead of time, so they shouldn't demand too much attention when time is against you. By varying your daily offering, you add an element of surprise and hopefully your efforts will pay off – there's nothing more frustrating than when a lunchbox returns home with its contents untouched.

Mini Pasties

PREPARATION TIME *10 minutes, plus 15 minutes soaking*

COOKING TIME *35 minutes* **FREEZING** *suitable* **MAKES** *6*

These mini pasties make a great addition to a lunchbox or picnic and are the right size for toddlers to hold. They can also be served warm for supper with new potatoes and vegetables. The flaky puff-pastry triangles encase a rich mixture of soya mince (or lean beef mince) and vegetables – make plenty, they'll go quickly'

1 Put the soya mince in a bowl and cover with boiling water. Add the yeast extract and stir until dissolved. Leave the soya for 15 minutes, until rehydrated. Meanwhile, steam or boil the potatoes and carrots until tender.

2 Heat the oil in a pan and sauté the onion for 5 minutes. Add the garlic and sauté for a further minute, stirring occasionally, until the onion has softened.

3 Add the cooked carrot and potato, the parsley, soya mince (and any soaking liquid), passata and soy sauce to the pan. Stir thoroughly, season with pepper to taste, and cook for 10 minutes, or until the mixture is quite dry.

4 Preheat the oven to 200°C/400°F/Gas Mark 6. Place the pastry on a work surface and cut into 6 x 10-cm/4-in squares. Place a heaped teaspoon of the

INGREDIENTS
25 g/1 oz dried soya mince (look for one that is GM free)
½ tsp yeast extract
1 small potato, peeled and diced
1 small carrot, peeled and diced
1 tsp vegetable oil
1 small onion, finely chopped
1 clove garlic, crushed
1 tbsp finely chopped fresh parsley
2 tbsp passata
1 tbsp soy sauce
freshly ground black pepper
375 g/13 oz ready-rolled puff pastry, defrosted if frozen
1 egg, beaten, to glaze

filling in the centre of each pastry square. Brush the edges with the beaten egg and fold the pastry in half to make a triangle. Seal the edges with a fork, then repeat to make 5 more pasties.

❺ Place the pasties on a lightly greased baking sheet, brush with the remaining egg and make a small air hole in the top using a skewer. Bake for 15–20 minutes, or until risen and golden.

Guacamole

PREPARATION TIME *5 minutes* **FREEZING** *unsuitable* **SERVES** *2–4*

This creamy dip is simple to prepare and makes a great filling for warm tortillas, pitta bread or sandwiches. Although the lemon juice helps the avocado to retain its colour, the guacamole is best eaten within a few hours of making.

❶ Place the avocado in a bowl and add the lemon juice, garlic and tomato (if using). Mash with a fork until smooth and creamy.

INGREDIENTS
1 ripe avocado, peeled, stoned and roughly chopped
juice of ½ lemon
1 small clove garlic, crushed
1 tomato, skinned, seeded and diced (optional)

Pink Pasta Salad

PREPARATION TIME *5 minutes* **COOKING TIME** *10 minutes*
FREEZING *unsuitable* **MAKES** *2–4 portions*

There is now a plethora of different pasta shapes to choose from, which adds to the fun and the appeal of this quick and easy salad. Use the prawns or salmon only if the salad can be refrigerated prior to lunchtime. If not, add diced red pepper and halved black grapes, which taste just as good.

❶ Cook the pasta according to the instructions on the packet, until the pasta is tender, then drain well.

❷ Mix together the mayonnaise and ketchup in a bowl and add the pasta, prawns and tomatoes. Line a container with lettuce leaves and spoon the pasta salad into the middle.

INGREDIENTS
85 g/3 oz pasta shapes of your choice
2 tbsp mayonnaise
1 tbsp tomato ketchup
55 g/2 oz cooked prawns or canned pink salmon, mashed (optional)
3 cherry tomatoes, quartered
lettuce leaves, optional

Cheese Twists

PREPARATION TIME *5 minutes* **COOKING TIME** *12 minutes*
FREEZING *suitable* **MAKES** *20 twists*

These savoury twists have a delicious cheesy flavour and are very tasty. They can be dipped into houmus.

INGREDIENTS
butter or margarine, for greasing
85 g/3 oz Gruyère cheese, grated
½ tsp paprika
375 g/13 oz ready-rolled puff pastry, defrosted if frozen
1 egg, beaten

1. Preheat the oven to 200°C/400°F/ Gas Mark 6. Grease a large baking sheet.

2. Mix together the Gruyère cheese and paprika and sprinkle over the sheet of puff pastry. Fold the puff pastry in half and roll out a little to seal the edges.

3. Cut the pastry into long 1-cm/½-in wide strips, then cut each strip in half and gently twist. Place on the prepared baking sheet. Brush with beaten egg and bake for 10–12 minutes, or until crisp and golden. Allow to cool on a wire rack.

Sandwiches

- Bagel with cream cheese and yeast extract
- Peanut butter with strawberry jam
- Peanut butter with mashed banana
- Sliced cooked chicken with grated apple and mayonnaise
- Chicken and mashed banana
- Mashed tuna, avocado with mayonnaise and a squeeze of lemon juice
- Houmus, diced tomato and chopped hard-boiled egg
- Sliced grilled bacon, chopped hard-boiled egg and mayonnaise
- Ham, mashed pineapple chunks and cottage cheese
- Cheese scones with bacon and cream cheese
- Vegetarian sausages with tomato
- Ciabatta with a wedge of omelette
- Ciabatta with pesto, mozzarella cheese and tomato

ABOVE *Healthy snacks and packed lunches will actually satisfy your child's appetite, and will not provide the 'false energy' feeling that very sugary foods produce.*

- Sardine paté and cucumber
- Pitta bread with couscous, houmus and mint
- Pitta bread pizzas

Snacks

- Raisin muffins with cream cheese
- Rice cakes with chocolate spread and sliced banana
- Nuts and raisins
- Breadsticks and dip
- Crumpets with strawberry jam and cream cheese
- Mini pitta breads spread with garlic butter and sprinkled with grated cheese and grilled
- Tortilla
- Flapjacks
- Malt loaf or fruit bread
- Fruit jelly with fresh fruit
- Houmus with sticks of carrot, cucumber and celery

Lemon Barley Water

PREPARATION TIME *5 minutes* **COOKING TIME** *35 minutes*

FREEZING *suitable* **MAKES** *1.7 litres/3 pints*

This home-made lemon drink is very refreshing on a hot day and is great for when your child has friends to play. It has less sugar than many shop-bought versions.

INGREDIENTS
225 g/8 oz pearl barley
1.7 litres/3 pints water
grated rind of 1 lemon
55 g/2 oz golden caster sugar
juice of 2 lemons

1. Rinse the barley under cold running water, then place in a large saucepan. Cover with water and bring to the boil. Reduce the heat and simmer for 30 minutes, skimming off any froth that may appear from time to time. Remove the pan from the heat.

2. Add the lemon rind and sugar to the pan, stir well until the sugar has dissolved and leave to cool. Strain, then add the lemon juice. Serve chilled.

VARIATIONS

Substitute orange rind and juice for lemon rind and juice.

Strawberry & Banana Shake

PREPARATION TIME *5 minutes* **FREEZING** *suitable* **SERVES** *2 adults*

This creamy fruity drink can be transformed into delicious lollies if it is frozen. You can use other fruit combinations too.

1. Put the bananas, strawberries, wheatgerm and yogurt in a blender and process for a minute, or until smooth and creamy. Pour into glasses and serve.

INGREDIENTS
2 bananas, quartered
225 g/8 oz strawberries, hulled and halved if large
1 tbsp wheatgerm or oatmeal
500 g/1 lb 2 oz natural live yogurt

Wiggly Noodle Soup

PREPARATION TIME *5 minutes* **COOKING TIME** *8 minutes*

FREEZING *suitable* **SERVES** *4 adults*

Quick, nutritious and fun, this soup can be messy, so be prepared! Miso is made from soya beans, which can be bought in paste form, although here I've gone for convenience and opted for instant miso soup that simply requires the addition of water.

INGREDIENTS
200 g/7 oz egg noodles
1 litre/1¾ pints instant miso soup
1 tbsp dark soy sauce
115 g/4 oz mangetout, thinly sliced diagonally
1 carrot, peeled and cut into fine strips
2 spring onions, finely sliced (optional)
1 tbsp toasted sesame seeds (optional)
salt and freshly ground black pepper

❶ Bring a large pan of water to the boil, add the noodles and cook according to the instructions on the packet, until the noodles are just tender. Drain the noodles in a colander. Rinse under cold running water, then drain again and set aside.

❷ Put the miso soup in a large saucepan and bring to the boil, then add the soy sauce.

❸ Reduce the heat and add the mangetout, carrot and spring onions, if using, and simmer for 3 minutes, or until the vegetables are just tender. Season to taste.

❹ Divide the noodles between four bowls and pour in the soup. Sprinkle with the sesame seeds.

Honey Salmon Kebabs

PREPARATION TIME *5 minutes, plus 1 hour marinating*

COOKING TIME *5 minutes* **FREEZING** *unsuitable* **SERVES** *4 adults*

The honey-based marinade gives a wonderful, sweet, caramel flavour and glossy coating to the cubes of salmon. While kebabs are fun, do take care when giving them to children. If you use wooden skewers, soak them in water to stop them burning.

INGREDIENTS
4 boneless salmon fillets, each about 140 g/ 5 oz, skinned and cut into 2-cm/¾-in cubes
1 tbsp toasted sesame seeds (optional)

MARINADE
2 tbsp runny honey
1 tbsp soy sauce
1 tbsp olive oil
1 tsp toasted sesame oil

❶ Mix together the ingredients for the marinade in a shallow dish. Add the salmon and stir to coat the fish in the marinade. Leave to marinate in the refrigerator for 1 hour, turning the fish occasionally.

❷ Preheat the grill to high. Thread the cubes of salmon onto 8 skewers. Line a grill rack with foil and place the skewers on top. Brush the salmon with the marinade and grill for 3–5 minutes, turning the skewers occasionally, until cooked.

❸ While the salmon is cooking, put the remaining marinade in a small saucepan and heat for a few minutes until it has reduced and thickened.

❹ Serve the kebabs with rice. Spoon the reduced marinade over the salmon and sprinkle with sesame seeds, if using.

Sunny Rice

PREPARATION TIME *10 minutes* **COOKING TIME** *30 minutes*

FREEZING *suitable* **SERVES** *4 adults*

This comforting, lightly spiced rice dish is topped with slices of hard-boiled egg for extra goodness. Make sure you choose undyed smoked fish, not the artificially coloured, yellow variety.

INGREDIENTS
450 g/1 lb undyed smoked haddock or cod fillets
450 ml/16 fl oz water
225 g/8 oz basmati rice, rinsed
1 bay leaf
2 cloves
4 tbsp butter
55 g/2 oz frozen petit pois
1 tsp garam masala
½ tsp ground turmeric
2 tbsp chopped flat-leaved parsley
4 hard-boiled eggs, quartered
freshly ground black pepper

❶ Put the haddock in a large frying pan and pour enough milk or water over the fish to just cover it. Poach the fish for 5 minutes, or until cooked and opaque. Remove the haddock from the pan and flake the fish, carefully removing the skin and any bones. Discard the remainder of the poaching liquid.

❷ Meanwhile, place the rice in a saucepan and cover with 475 ml/16 fl oz water, then add the bay leaf and cloves. Bring to the boil, then reduce the heat and simmer, covered, for 15 minutes, or until the water has been absorbed and the rice is tender. Discard the bay leaf and cloves. Set aside the covered pan.

❸ Melt the butter over a gentle heat in the cleaned frying pan, then add the peas and cook for 2 minutes, or until tender. Stir in the garam masala and turmeric and cook for another minute.

❹ Stir in the haddock and rice and mix well until they are coated in the spiced butter.

❺ Season and heat through for 1–2 minutes. Stir in the parsley and top with the hard-boiled eggs just before serving.

Chicken, Apple & Nut Salad

PREPARATION TIME *5 minutes* **COOKING TIME** *1 minute*
FREEZING *unsuitable* **SERVES** *2 adults*

The creamy dressing and the sweetness of the apple add to the child-appeal of this crunchy salad. I've included spring onion, but you can easily leave it out without detriment to the flavour.

❶ Toast the pine kernels in a dry frying pan until lightly golden.

❷ Toss the apple in the lemon juice to prevent the flesh from discolouring. Place the apple and any leftover lemon juice in a bowl with the chicken, celery and spring onion, if using. Add the toasted pine kernels.

❸ Mix together the mayonnaise and yogurt and spoon the dressing over the salad. Mix well to coat the salad in the dressing.

INGREDIENTS
1 tbsp pine kernels
1 red-skinned apple, cored and diced
1 tbsp lemon juice
175 g/6 oz cooked chicken breast, skinned and diced
1 celery stick, finely chopped
1 spring onion, finely chopped (optional)

DRESSING
2 tbsp mayonnaise
3 tbsp natural yogurt

Christmas Pie

PREPARATION TIME *10 minutes* **COOKING TIME** *25 minutes*

FREEZING *suitable* **MAKES** *4 adults*

These individual golden puff-pastry pies are full of flavours that are reminiscent of the festive season.

INGREDIENTS

- 375 g/13 oz ready-rolled puff pastry, defrosted if frozen
- 2 skinless turkey breasts, each weighing about 115 g/4 oz
- 2 tbsp redcurrant chutney or cranberry jelly
- 150 g/5½ oz sage and onion stuffing
- 1 egg, beaten
- salt and freshly ground black pepper

1. Preheat the oven to 200°C/400°F/Gas Mark 6. Lay out the pastry on a lightly floured work surface. Divide the pastry into four pieces.

2. Season the turkey breasts and cut each one into two. Arrange the turkey fillets on top of the pastry, leaving a border around the edge, then spoon over the chutney. Divide the stuffing in four and place it on top.

3. Fold the long edges of the pastry together and seal the top with water, then fold in the ends and seal. Repeat with the remaining three parcels. Cut any remaining pastry into holly shapes and place on top of each parcel. Brush each pie with beaten egg and place on a lightly greased baking sheet.

4. Bake for 25 minutes, or until the pastry is golden and the turkey is cooked inside.

Baby Burgers

PREPARATION TIME *10 minutes* **COOKING TIME** *30 minutes*
FREEZING *suitable* **MAKES** *10 burgers*

There's something very appealing about bite-sized foods and these mini burgers are no exception, fitting perfectly into those sesame or poppy seed baby rolls you can now buy. These burgers are perfect for little hands to hold and are easy to eat.

INGREDIENTS
40 g/1½ oz fresh wholemeal breadcrumbs
1 tsp dried oregano
1 onion, grated
1 carrot, peeled and grated
1 clove garlic, crushed
425 g/15 oz lean beef mince
1 tbsp tomato purée
1 egg, beaten
vegetable oil, for frying
salt and freshly ground black pepper

TO SERVE
mini burger buns
lettuce leaves
sliced tomato
mayonnaise or relish

1. Place all the ingredients for the burgers, except the oil, in a large bowl and mix together with your hands until combined. Season, then shape the mixture into small balls, using your hands. Set aside in the refrigerator for 15 minutes.

2. Heat enough oil to cover the bottom of a large heavy-based frying pan and fry the meatballs, for 3–5 minutes, turning them occasionally, until cooked through and browned.

3. Serve the burgers in a small bun with lettuce, sliced tomato and mayonnaise or relish.

Chinese Omelette Roll

PREPARATION TIME *5 minutes* **COOKING TIME** *8 minutes*
FREEZING *unsuitable* **SERVES** *4 adults*

A thin, golden omelette makes a remarkably good wrapping for stir-fried vegetables.

INGREDIENTS
115 g/4 oz broccoli florets, cut into small pieces
2 tbsp groundnut oil
1 clove garlic
1-cm/½-in piece of fresh root ginger, finely grated
1 small red pepper, seeded and diced
85 g/3 oz white cabbage, finely shredded
85 g/3 oz beansprouts
2 tbsp black bean sauce
4 eggs, lightly beaten
salt and freshly ground black pepper

❶ Blanch the broccoli in boiling water for 2 minutes, until slightly softened. Drain the broccoli, then refresh under cold running water.

❷ Heat half the oil in a wok or frying pan. Add the garlic, ginger, red pepper, cabbage and broccoli and stir-fry for 3 minutes, tossing the vegetables constantly to prevent them sticking.

❸ Add the beansprouts and stir-fry for a further minute, then add the black bean sauce, stir and heat through. Remove from the heat and cover the wok or pan to keep the stir-fry warm.

❹ Season the beaten eggs. Heat a little of the remaining oil in a small frying pan and add a quarter of the beaten egg. Swirl the egg to cover the base of the pan. Cook until set, then turn the omelette out on to a plate and keep warm while you make three more omelettes.

❺ Spoon the vegetable stir-fry along the centre of the omelette and roll it up. Cut it crossways.

VARIATIONS

Prawns or chicken make a delicious addition to the stir-fried vegetables. If using strips of chicken, cook them in Step 2, until browned, before adding the garlic and ginger. Add the prawns with the garlic in Step 2.

Green Giant Pasta

PREPARATION TIME *10 minutes* **COOKING TIME** *15 minutes*
FREEZING *suitable* **SERVES** *4 adults*

I've included a recipe for fresh pesto, but the ready-made variety can be used if preferred or if time is short. Pesto is a real favourite with many children and just a spoonful transforms pasta or rice.

INGREDIENTS
375 g/13 oz linguine, spaghetti or tagliatelle
8 new potatoes, halved or quartered, if large
2 tsp olive oil
55 g/2 oz frozen petit pois
1–2 tbsp pine kernels, toasted in a dry frying pan

PESTO
55 g/2 oz fresh basil leaves
2 cloves garlic, crushed
40 g/1½ oz pine kernels
125 ml/4 fl oz olive oil, plus extra for drizzling
4 tbsp freshly grated Parmesan cheese
salt and freshly ground black pepper

1. First make the pesto. Place the basil, garlic and pine kernels in a blender and process until finely chopped. Gradually add the oil and then the Parmesan cheese and blend to a coarse purée. Season to taste. Spoon the pesto into a jar with a lid. Pour over extra olive oil to cover. Use immediately or store in the refrigerator for up to a week.

2. Cook the pasta according to the instructions on the packet, until the pasta is just tender, then drain, reserving 1–2 tablespoons of the cooking water.

3. Meanwhile, cook the potatoes in boiling water for 10 minutes, or until tender. Cut the potato into bite-sized cubes.

4. Heat the oil in a large saucepan, then add 4 tablespoons of pesto, the cooked potatoes and peas. Heat the pesto mixture for a few minutes, then season to taste. Add the pasta and the reserved cooking water if it appears too dry. Heat through and mix in the pine kernels.

5. Serve sprinkled with cheese.

Fresh Fruit Sticks

PREPARATION TIME *10 minutes* **COOKING TIME** *15 minutes*

FREEZING *unsuitable* **SERVES** *4 adults*

Children can help to assemble these colourful, vitamin-rich fruit sticks, but they do need adult supervision if they are very young. The fruit sticks can be grilled or barbecued and are excellent served with a dollop of thick natural yogurt or a good-quality vanilla ice cream. Wooden skewers are preferable, but do soak them for 10 minutes beforehand to prevent them burning.

❶ Preheat the grill to high and line the grill pan with foil. Arrange the fruit along the wooden skewers.

❷ Heat the honey or maple syrup in a small saucepan until runny and brush liberally over the kebabs using a pastry brush or your fingers, if you prefer.

❸ Grill for 5–8 minutes, or until the fruit softens and the honey or syrup begins to caramelise.

INGREDIENTS

Choose from a selection of fresh fruit: pineapples, mangoes, bananas, kiwi, peaches and oranges are best, cut into 1-cm/½-in chunks

runny honey or maple syrup, for brushing

Little Jack Horner Pudding

PREPARATION TIME *10 minutes* **COOKING TIME** *30 minutes*
FREEZING *unsuitable* **SERVES** *4 adults*

This warming plum batter pudding is similar to the classic French dessert clafoutis. It is best served hot with cream.

1. Preheat the oven to 200°C/400°F/Gas Mark 6.

2. Beat the eggs, egg yolk and sugar in a large bowl until light and frothy. Stir in the vanilla essence and flour with a wooden spoon and beat until smooth.

3. Mix together the melted butter, soured cream and milk and add to the bowl. Gently stir until everything is combined.

4. Arrange the plums in the bottom of a lightly buttered 20 cm/8 in ovenproof dish, then pour the egg mixture over the fruit. Bake for 25–30 minutes, or until risen and set.

INGREDIENTS
2 eggs
1 egg yolk
85 g/3 oz caster sugar
1 tsp vanilla essence
55 g/2 oz plain flour, sifted
40 g/1½ oz unsalted butter, melted, plus extra for greasing
100 ml/3½ fl oz soured cream
50 ml/2 fl oz full-cream milk
3 plums, stoned and roughly chopped

Gingerbread People

PREPARATION TIME *10 minutes*

COOKING TIME *12 minutes*

FREEZING *unsuitable*

MAKES *6 people, or more depending on the size of the cutter*

INGREDIENTS
175 g/6 oz plain flour
2 tsp ground ginger
½ tsp bicarbonate of soda
55 g/2 oz butter or margarine
85 g/3 oz soft brown sugar
2 tbsp golden syrup
1 egg, beaten
TO DECORATE
Royal icing, piping consistency
Smarties or raisins

Children love helping to make these golden gingerbread men and women.

❶ Preheat the oven to 190°C/375°F/Gas Mark 5. Sift the flour, ginger and bicarbonate of soda into a large mixing bowl. Add the butter and rub into the flour with your fingers until the mixture resembles fine breadcrumbs. Mix in the sugar.

❷ Warm the syrup in a small saucepan until runny, then add to the flour mixture with the beaten egg. Mix to form a soft dough, then knead lightly until smooth. If the dough is too sticky, add a little extra flour.

❸ Roll out the dough on a lightly floured work surface then, using a cutter, make the gingerbread people. Place on a lightly greased baking sheet and cook for 10 minutes, or until just crisp and golden. Allow to cool.

❹ Pipe small blobs of icing to make a face and buttons on each person. Use the Smarties or raisins to form eyes and buttons.

Passion Cake Squares

PREPARATION TIME *15 minutes* **COOKING TIME** *1 hour*

FREEZING *unsuitable* **MAKES** *1 cake*

This moist, light carrot cake couldn't be easier to make and is a delicious way to encourage your child to eat vegetables!

INGREDIENTS
225 g/8 oz self-raising flour
pinch of salt
1 tsp ground cinnamon
1 tsp ground nutmeg
225 g/8 oz light muscovado sugar
225 g/8 oz carrots, peeled and finely grated
100 g/3½ oz dried, ready-to-eat dates, roughly chopped
3 eggs, lightly beaten
175 ml/6 fl oz sunflower oil

ICING
115 g/4 oz cream cheese
4 tbsp butter
1 tsp vanilla essence
200 g/7 oz icing sugar

1. Preheat the oven to 180°C/350°F/Gas Mark 4. Lightly grease a 20-cm/8-in square cake tin and line the base with greaseproof paper.

2. Sift the flour and salt into a large mixing bowl. Add the spices, sugar, carrots and dates and mix well until combined.

3. Stir together the beaten eggs and oil, then pour into the mixing bowl and beat until thoroughly combined.

4. Pour the slightly lumpy mixture into the prepared tin and bake for 1 hour, or until a skewer inserted into the centre of the cake comes out clean. Leave for 5 minutes, then carefully turn out the cake and allow to cool.

5. To make the icing, beat the cream cheese, butter and vanilla essence together until smooth and creamy. Beat in the sugar and store the icing in the refrigerator for 20 minutes to harden slightly. Spread the icing over the cake and cut it into small squares.

VARIATIONS

Substitute finely grated courgettes for the carrot and add 1 tbsp pine kernels or chopped walnuts.

Useful Websites and Organisations

These provide information on childcare and nutrition, and can help you if you have any questions or concerns.

USEFUL WEBSITES

kidshealth.org
A useful site with sections on feeding your toddler: feeding your 1–2 year old, deciphering food labels, healthy mealtime habits, nutrients your child needs and packing school lunches.

www.allhealth.com
This site gives information on school-age nutrition, an area that often worries parents because their children come under different influences when they start full-time education.

www.abcparenting.com
General information on feeding toddlers and coping with their first time at school.

babyparenting.about.com
Information on child nutrition and health.

www.babycenter.com
Information on toddler behaviour and development, toddler health, feeding, nutrition and breastfeeding your toddler.

www.kidsource.com
Addresses health and diseases issues, and the correct kind of preventive care. Also deals with nutritional questions.

www.drgreene.com/toddlers.html
Information on the effect of sugar on behaviour and the value of vegetables – plus advice on handling temper tantrums.

www.uri.edu/coopext/efnep/toddlers/toddler.p4.html
Information on the characteristics of the toddler, feeding the toddler, appropriate foods and amounts for toddlers and a guide to the appropriate serving sizes.

www.findarticles.com
A collection of recipes for nutritious and tasty children's breakfasts to replace sugar-coated cereal and milk.

www.pampers.com
Offers tips for enticing toddlers at every developmental stage to participate in meals.

www.parentsoup.com
Find answers to common questions about toddler nutrition. Includes advice for parents of picky eaters and tips on weaning.

www.parentsplace.com
Expert advice on issues such as lactose intolerance, pickiness and food allergies. Also contains toddler nutrition guidelines, information on picky eaters, feeding guidelines, nutritional guidelines, vegetarian issues, allergies and sensitivities and food safety.

www.diapernet.com/diqa/diqas19.htm
Encouraging toddlers to eat a variety of foods: suggestions from parents on getting toddlers to stray from their favourite foods.

www.thecybermom.com
Features resources on tons of toddler-related subjects, including useful information on food preferences and picky eating.

www.mothersnature.com
Post a question about toddler behaviour or development or scan the boards for advice on a range of topics.

www.toddlerstoday.com
News related to toddlers, along with articles, an expert Q&A and parent diaries.

USEFUL ORGANISATIONS

Association of Breastfeeding Mothers
abm@clara.net
http://home.clara.net/abm/
Offers breastfeeding advice and information, and trains breastfeeding counsellors.

Beyond the Baby Blues
www.babyblues.freeserve.co.uk
Offers an easily accessible, confidential support network for mothers who are suffering from postnatal depression.

Centre for Pregnancy Nutrition
pregnancy.nutrition@sheffield.ac.uk
Helpline: (+44) 0114 2424084

Fathers Direct
www.fathersdirect.com
mail@fathersdirect.com
Promotes close and positive relationships between men and their children from infancy. Aims to break down barriers that exist in society that make it difficult for fathers to develop such relationships with their children.

Parentline Plus
www.parentline.co.uk
Helpline: (+44) 0808 800 2222
Offers support to anyone who is parenting a child – the child's parents, step-parents, grandparents, and foster parents. Provides a range of information.

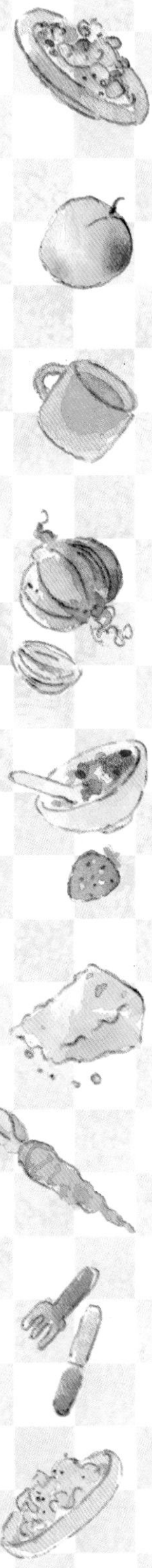

Index

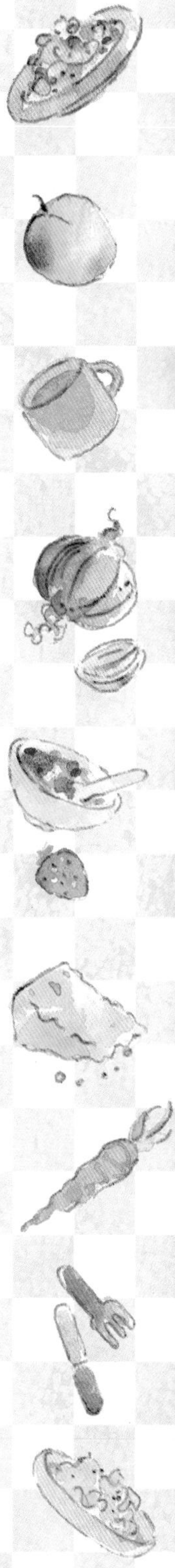

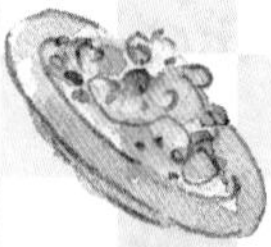

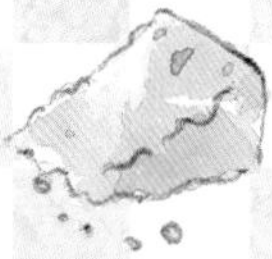
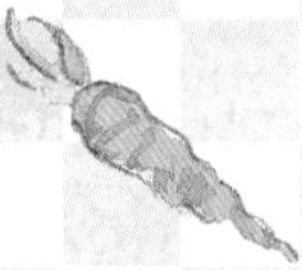

Acknowledgements

The author would like to thank the following:

The Institute of Child Health, London; The Health Education Authority, London; The Department of Health, London.

The publishers would like to thank the following for permission to reproduce copyright material: Bubbles: pp. 6, 36, 39, 69; Getty Stone: pp. 4, 7, 8; Image Bank: pp. 9, 10, 13, 24, 37, 66; Superstock: pp. 5, 14.